Other Books by Frank McKinney

Dead Fred, Flying Lunchboxes, and the Good Luck Circle

Burst This! Frank McKinney's Bubble-Proof Real Estate Strategies

*Frank McKinney's Maverick Approach to Real Estate Success:
How You Can Go From a $50,000 Fixer-Upper
to a $100 Million Mansion*

Make It BIG! 49 Secrets for Building a Life of Extreme Success

the Tap

the Tap

FRANK McKINNEY

Health Communications, Inc.
Deerfield Beach, Florida

www.hcibooks.com

Library of Congress Cataloging-in-Publication Data

McKinney Frank.
    The tap / Frank McKinney.
      p. cm.
    Includes bibliographical references and index.
    ISBN-13: 978-0-7573-1384-4 (hardcover)
    ISBN-10: 0-7573-1384-1 (hardcover)
    1. Success—Psychological aspects.   2. Success—religious aspects—Christianity.   I. Title.
BF637.S8M343 2009
158—dc22

                                                      200802731

Publisher: Health Communications, Inc.
           3201 S.W. 15th Street
           Deerfield Beach, FL 33442–8190

Some people's names have been changed to protect their privacy; however, all the stories in this book are true, and wherever first and last names appear, these are individual's actual names. In all cases, the author has done his best to accurately represent real experiences with The Tap.

Bible passages are quoted from the New International Version.

This book was printed on recycled paper.

The Leadership in Energy and Environmental Design (LEED) Green Building Rating System™ of the U.S. Green Building Council encourages and accelerates global adoption of sustainable green LEED building and development practices through the creation and implementation of universally understood and accepted tools and performance criteria. This book is part of Frank McKinney's efforts to educate the public about these practices and standards.

Cover design by Erik Hollander, HollanderDesignLab.com
Interior design and formatting by Lawna Patterson Oldfield

To all those who are
feeling or recognizing The Tap
for the first time:
may your awareness of and
sensitivity to life's Tap Moments
enlighten you to become the
responsible steward
God desires and rewards.

From everyone who has been given much, much more will be demanded; and from the one who has been entrusted with much, much more will be asked.

—LUKE 12:48

CONTENTS

Acknowledgments xi

Introduction: "In the Beginning . . ." xvii

Part One: Feel The Tap

One   Tap Into Eternal Success 5

Two   Deserve What You Ask For 27

Three   It's No "Secret" 47

Four   Tap Moments: The Test, a Touch, and
God's Knockout Punch 63

Five   Get Off Your Knees and Start Walking.................87

Part Two: Act on The Tap

Six   Say Yes More Than No 115

Seven   Why Not Drive a Purple Yugo?.........................127

Eight   Pack This in Your Lunch Pail............................145

Nine   The Microwave Prayer 159

Ten   Think Fast, Act Faster 163

Part Three: Break Through With The Tap: Dance!

Eleven   Often Happy, Seldom Satisfied............................183

Twelve   Doing the Opposite Attracts..............................197

Thirteen   The Eternal, Upward Spiral 215

Fourteen   Strap Yourself In: Prepare for a
              Rapid Rate of Ascent......................................227

Fifteen   The White Line from Hell to Heaven..............245

Notes...268

About the Author...273

Index..276

Other Exciting Offerings from Frank McKinney............280

ACKNOWLEDGMENTS

W HEN YOU'VE WRITTEN A few books, it becomes more challenging to recognize new people who have contributed to your success or, more appropriately, contributed to the material and message found in a new work.

In my 2006 bestseller, *Frank McKinney's Maverick Approach*, I began by acknowledging those who contributed to my twenty-year journey of becoming known as a real estate "artist," creating the most beautiful oceanfront estate homes in the world and making markets where they hadn't existed before. I love to write, and that list grew to more than 145 very important people. It's clear that I've needed much assistance along the way. Where to stop? I'm grateful to so many people that the list took up eight pages.

The acknowledgments in my first bestseller, *Make It BIG! 49 Secrets for Building a Life of Extreme Success,* related to those who'd helped shape the way I looked at life in general, from grade school teachers on to the publishers of *Make It BIG!* Again, I created a fairly important list, adding up to five pages.

This time, I reflect on a life approach that revolves and evolves around *The Tap*, which took me decades to understand and truly apply. It's fair to say that my own contributions to this world can be broken down into two phases, pre- and post-Tap.

So I'd like to acknowledge those who've contributed to my life post-Tap, and who've helped me develop the very concept of The Tap.

If I trace the origin of my first feeling for The Tap, it goes back to the late 1990s, when I began serving meals out of the back of a beat-up old van to people who were homeless. So I must start with those associated with The Caring Kitchen, a small organization that still runs a soup kitchen and homeless assistance center in Delray Beach, Florida. There was Bonnie Cipriani, who introduced me as a volunteer and drove me into the back alleys to serve hot meals for the first time. Just witnessing her pour out unconditional love was so inspiring. Juanita Bryant Goode, the program director, was always so inclusive and treated the poor with so much compassion. I want to acknowledge Pam Cahoon, who remains the executive director of C.R.O.S. (Christians Reaching Out to Society) Ministries, the organization that oversees The Caring Kitchen, and who's been on the Caring House Project Foundation board of directors for nearly ten years. Most impactful, though, were the early conversations I had with many people living on the streets, under a bridge, or in their car. You had no idea the seeds you were planting.

When I felt it was time to implement a larger version of The Tap through the formation of our foundation, I needed a board of directors who knew more than I, and I was and am fortunate to be surrounded by wise men and women. I want to thank our current board members,

Dennis Moran, Ezra Krieg, Pam Cahoon, Marti Forman, Scott Elk, Jim Toner, John Dessauer, David Dweck, Joe Silk, Addie Green, Bob McKinney, and my wife, Nilsa McKinney. Many have been associated with our mission for nearly a decade. They've tapped thousands of souls, none more deeply than mine. I also want to thank all past board members for their years of tirelessly serving those most desperately poor and homeless.

The larger The Tap, the more front office support I've needed to implement it. Our impact would never have grown so significantly had it not been for the Caring House Project Foundation executive director Kimberley Trombly-Burmeister, our vice president Lori Tanner, and our operations manager Anne Lee.

The breadth of The Tap's impact would never have been so significant if not for donors to our Caring House Project Foundation. From the $8.15 donations made to buy a chicken for a village, to the donors who have given hundreds of thousands of dollars to build entire villages, to you and others who have bought my books (a part of each purchase is actually a donation to the Caring House Project Foundation): I wish to sincerely thank everyone for sharing your blessings.

I've learned much of what I know through an acute ability to observe, then extrapolate, behavior I've wanted to emulate. As a young adult, watching others who displayed the characteristics that I looked up to was vital to the formation of my character. I've often said that if ever the church convenes "Vatican III," and as part of the agenda they allow married men to be priests, then I'd be the first to sign up. Why? Because much of the behavior I've witnessed in good priests and other religious leaders, regardless of faith, I try to copy.

I learned much from Brother David Downey (deceased), a Benedictine monk who was the prefect at The Abbey School of the Holy Cross Abbey Monastery in Canon City, Colorado, during my junior year of high school. That was way pre-Tap. Although he asked me to leave (kicked me out), we stayed in touch. As I grew into an adult, watching him care for the migrant farm workers and conduct his prison ministry while keeping stronger than the Brawny towel guy by baling hay on The Abbey farm, had an impact on me. To be close to him, we even bought a vacation home in the little town.

Succeeding in the business of life means having it all and being acutely aware of your responsibility to share it. There have been those few I've admired who seem to possess both the ability and understanding to do so. The first that comes to mind is my personal mentor, Rich DeVos. I mentioned him in my first two books, too. His influence on my now "tapped" life is inescapable, and I wrote about him throughout this book. I thank God for every minute I'm able to share in Rich's presence.

I want to thank all of the hardworking people at HCI Books, my publisher. Their belief in *The Tap* and willingness to publish not only this book, but two others I wrote and they released simultaneously, speaks volumes. I specifically want to thank Peter Vegso, Thomas Sand, Pat Holdsworth, Paola Fernandez, Kim Weiss, Carol Rosenberg, Michele Matrisciani, Andrea Gold, Kelly Maragni, Lori Golden, Sean Geary, Mike Briggs, Craig Jarvie, Christine Zambrano, Sidney Stevens, and Manuel Saez.

Books don't sell themselves. Circulating the message of *The Tap* around the globe is a large undertaking. I want to thank Jane Grant, my publicist from Pierson Grant Public Relations, for her tireless efforts and enthusiasm for this work.

I want to thank Erik Hollander for his skillful work on the book cover. Take a look; it's simply amazing. I also want to sincerely thank Karen Risch for her invaluable input in this book. Having her come into my life and help me to develop the concepts found here will result in a lifelong Tap Moment.

Many of my Tap Moments have been experienced with my family, as I'm sure yours have been or will be. I want to thank my four sisters, Martie, Marlen, Madeleine, and Heather. I especially want to acknowledge my best friend and brother Bob (or "Chook," as I call him) for sharing thousands of hours of Tap-Moment conversations with me.

My mother, Katie, represents the epitome and embodiment of The Tap. I want to thank her for allowing me to see the compassionate and caring side of life. Thank you for being so patient.

My wife, Nilsa, and daughter, Laura, are more than Tap Moments; they make up my tapped life. They've witnessed Tap Moments with me and helped me follow through on many of them, always encouraging me to expand the territory I've gained through The Tap. I love you both very much and look forward to many more taps as a small but powerful little family.

To live The Tap, you need accomplices. These are individuals whose lives are made better by your awareness of the impact that acting on a Tap Moment will have on them. I regularly pray to God that such people will be introduced to me so that I might act according to his will. I want to acknowledge and thank the thousands of men, women, and children I've had the good fortune to know through the Caring House Foundation: from Buster, Red, and Chainsaw, who lived in the first dollar-a-month houses we made available here in the United States, to the thousands of people of the self-sustaining villages of Haiti, Honduras, Nicaragua, Indonesia, and Africa. While it may appear as if you were the ones who were served, by your need I was served to strengthen and hone the concept of The Tap, so now others may reach out, as well. May God bless you in the way you've been a blessing to me.

INTRODUCTION

"In the Beginning"

W HENEVER WE REVEAL OUR artistry to the world, showcasing one of Frank McKinney & Company's magnificent, one-of-a-kind oceanfront estates for the first time, it's a complete spectacle. These grand unveiling events have become legendary, a theatrical assault on the senses belonging more on Broadway or the Las Vegas strip than on the soft, sandy beaches of South Florida. They're also the hottest ticket in town, with hundreds of media personnel, VIPs, and million-dollar brokers clamoring to attend.

On "opening night," we thoroughly set the stage, cloaking the mansion in drapery and uncovering it only after a dramatic flourish. Dressed as a sword-wielding pirate, I've descended on a 300-foot zip line stretched from chimney to water garden; I've appeared in a white suit, riding a jet ski through a cloud of smoke up onto the beach; we've had French soldiers storm the walls of the mansion in a re-enactment of Bastille Day; most recently, I dressed as a chivalrous knight, donned red and white velvet, and rappelled from a helicopter to land on a white horse, which I rode to escort partygoers to view our latest creation, known as Acqua Liana. Before we lift the drape, we present a show stopping finale of fireworks rivaling the biggest and best Fourth of July celebration. We always choreograph such a memorable scene that you might think there's no way a home can outshine the introduction, but the mansion always steals the show.

When we celebrated my twentieth anniversary of making markets in the real estate business, we planned another show-stopping event sure

A Theatrical Assault on the Senses

Here I am in one of my grand unveiling costumes, dressed as a swashbuckling pirate and ready to ride that 300-foot zip line over a crowd gathered below to the grounds of our palatial estate.

to top all previous efforts. I was preparing to jump my motorcycle over a full-scale replica of the first house I'd ever sold, a $50,000 fixer-upper I'd bought and renovated back in the late 1980s. The anniversary was a great excuse for me to pay tribute to one of my lifelong inspirations, the only living super hero I'd ever known, Evel Knievel. We were also playing on the word *launch*: I'd launch myself over a house that symbolized the beginning of my career and land on the spot where I was launching my next multimillion-dollar spec home, while at the same time we were launching my second book, *Frank McKinney's Maverick Approach.*

On the day of the event, a cold front headed our way. By the time we arrived to set up, I could see black clouds building to the north, lightning strikes all around us, and the wind beginning to blow sand into dunes.

About that time, my book-tour bus arrived, too—the same one Beyoncé Knowles had used in her last concert tour—now decked out with a giant image of my new book cover plastered on the side, which means the picture of my face was about four feet tall. Like the cherry on top of this party's sundae, this massive, rolling, Frank-McKinney-mansion-on-wheels billboard pulled up, the doors opened, and the driver stepped off.

He ignored the whipping wind and walked straight to me, extending his hand. "Howdy, I'm Tom Denman," he drawled. "I saw your picture on the side of the bus, and you're the only one 'round here with long hair, so I figgered you must be Frank."

That was my first introduction to Tom, a straight talker, a man in his seventies who (I'd later learn) had more than five million miles under his butt and fifty years behind the wheel. It was immediately apparent that it would take a lot to ruffle him, and I don't think the weather or anything else about the forthcoming festivities affected Tom much. (You might think my life sounds excessive or eccentric, but to Tom, I wasn't so remarkable. He's been driving superstars cross-country for decades, and according to him, all the wild stories you hear are absolutely true—and then some. By comparison, I must have seemed like Little Bo Peep herding her sheep on a tour of green pastures.)

I'd been curious to meet Tom, since we'd be spending the next two months together in close quarters. One of my concerns was that he wouldn't be too personable and would want things his way. That could have been rough, because I had definitive ideas about how I wanted the tour to unfold.

"Beautiful bus," I told him.

"Where do you want me to park 'er?" he asked.

This was as good a time as any to find out about him, so I told Tom exactly where I wanted him to put the bus. "If you don't mind," I added.

In a matter-of-fact tone, he replied, "Oh, no, it's gonna bottom out." He sized me up and then laid it on the line: "Ya need ta get me a backhoe in here. I'll put 'er wherever ya want 'er, but ya gotta make sure I got enough clearance."

"Yes, sir," I told him, and one Bobcat and a few dirt piles later, Tom drove the bus to its mark and parked it on a dime, right where I'd wanted it, so that when all our guests arrived, they'd have the opportunity to tour the bus on their way to the main event. That told me what I needed to know—the man had his own high standards and way of doing things, and he was also willing to do what I asked. I liked him.

But back to the wind and the rain and the impending motorcycle stunt. By the time we were ready for the jump, it was gusting, and the smoke machine we'd set up at the base of the landing ramp was blowing straight into my face and making it hard to see where I was going. Plus the take-off ramp was wet, and I hadn't practiced the jump under any special conditions. My wife, Nilsa, had gotten quiet. My daughter, Laura, was crying. My friends were telling me that I didn't have to do this and nobody would think any less of me if I didn't because I could slip and . . .

Despite the weather, with hands trembling and knees knocking against the gas tank, I jumped my Kawasaki over that house, landed on the ground where we're now in the process of creating an estate we plan to sell for $135 million, and kicked off my book tour for what was to become my second bestseller in less than five years.

That night, I also got my first glimpse of Tom's compassionate side. While I'd been reassuring Nilsa that we'd actually prepared the ramp for rain by applying nonskid paint, Tom had been genuinely concerned for my safety. He'd grown silent and paced back and forth a few times, just shaking his head at me when I said I had to follow through. No doubt the self-inflicted drama of the evening also formed his impression of me as a daredevil who loves risk and prefers to live on the edge. (I'm sure that also planted the seed for Tom to test my risk tolerance, but I'll get to that later.)

In the next year, Tom and I would spend a lot of time together. We drove to 23 cities in 58 days, where I made 110 appearances, did 212

Launch!

It was the ride of a lifetime: Jumping over a full-scale replica of the first home I ever sold, launching our new book, and landing on the site of Acqua Liana, one of our new oceanfront creations—all while paying homage to my hero, Evel Knievel. (Yes, that's me in the photo.)

bookstore drop-by signings, and covered 12,710 miles. As you can imagine, we had a lot of time on the road to talk, and as we talked, I cemented some of the central ideas you'll find in this book.

From Trapped to Tapped

"Hey, Frank, look at that guy," Tom said to me one day. "See his face?"

We were staring out the bus window on another rainy day as we rolled down the road somewhere outside Madison, Wisconsin. For a few minutes, we watched as car after car passed with drivers who appeared vacant and unfulfilled, as if they were trapped in an existence that didn't even come close to living up to their life's expectations. Not that you're supposed to get behind the wheel with a big grin on your face every day, but these people seemed so beaten down. It reminded me of the lyrics from an old Police song: ". . . packed like lemmings into shiny metal boxes, contestants in a suicidal race."

Tom observed, "You see a lot of people like that on the highway."

"I see a lot of people like that on the highway of life," I told him.

He knew what I meant. We'd talked before about how so many people clench their hands at ten and two, driving themselves straight to hell. Hell on earth, anyway. Tom had been there, too. In his twenties, he'd done his time as part-owner of a printing company and found it stifling. Driving a bus, on the other hand, represented total freedom for him. He felt for the people he imagined were spending their days doing something they didn't love and who lacked any real fire in their lives.

As we watched the cars go by, I reflected on the parade of people I'd met with the same expression on their faces.

Through the years, I've gotten to know quite a few men and women with that look, and they've shared their personal stories with me, particularly during luncheons that I regularly host in my infamous tree-house office overlooking the Atlantic Ocean. My guests have typically won the lunch with me by bidding on it at a charity auction or real estate event. Usually, they want to come mainly because the tree house has gotten a lot of press (a fair share of it controversial) and because I've earned a reputation as the "king of ready-made dream homes." In a word, they're curious.

Settling in for our meal, they frequently ask me how I can seem so grounded. Given that I'm supposed to be such a thrill seeker, they can't quite figure out why I'm not that adrenaline-fueled showman all the time. Since I'm in what most people consider an astronomically high-stakes business, they wonder how I keep a full head of hair and manage to sleep at all at night. They're fascinated by my risk tolerance. Every home I create is undertaken completely on speculation, meaning that I build it without a buyer in sight. I put multiple millions of dollars on the line and finish the home, right down to the gold-plated toothbrush in the bathroom, fine linens on the beds, and spa-grade towels in the closet. All of this is done with the belief, like in the movie *Field of Dreams,* that if I build it, they (buyers) will come. People are also puzzled by the dichotomy between my public image as the "real estate rock czar," with my mansions and long hair (shouldn't I be boozing it up and chasing women?) and my life as a private family man, which is a lot more like Ward Cleaver's than Tommy Lee's.

Yet there's a force that's ultimately far more powerful than their interest in me, which is their own sense that there's *something greater for them.* They come to believe that maybe I can help them figure out how to get there.

What starts out as a novelty luncheon often turns into a private confessional about how they long for more. "Something's missing," they tell me, expecting me to help them fill in the blanks. No matter what a person's net worth or level of professional accomplishment, whenever someone comes to my tree house seeking answers, it's because of one thing: **They don't feel they're succeeding at the level they desire in the business we're all in, which is the business of life.**

Maybe you've had the sense that there's something greater for you, too. Maybe that's why you picked up this book. Maybe when you saw the power represented by its cover, you thought, *Well, I could use some of what this guy's talking about. I'd like to experience The Tap, whatever that is.*

If so, you're a few steps ahead of my lunch guests, who usually hope I'll be able to give them some kind of secret to doing well for themselves. It's a special moment for me when someone asks how they can make more money, be more fit (lose weight), get more customers, have more time off, be more connected with family, or whatever their version of "more" may be. That's when I feel called to share what's been the greatest influence on my own sense of success and the central idea of the book you're holding in your hands right now: **Each of us is fortunate to be blessed with the ability to succeed at some level, not for our sole benefit, but so we may apply the results of our success to assist others.**

In other words, from those to whom much has been entrusted, much will be expected. The Bible counsels, "From everyone who has been given much, much more will be demanded; and from the one who has been entrusted with much, much more will be asked." Anyone who has the wherewithal to get to my tree house for a lunch—or to read this book, for that matter—has quite a lot, indeed. Each of us has the resources and ability to share something of ourselves with others, and to do it at whatever level makes sense for us in our lives right now.

When I wrote about this central idea in my first book, *Make It BIG!*, I dedicated all of Chapter 32 to the topic, and it became one of the two chapters that most resonated with hundreds of thousands of readers. (The other was Chapter 25, about strengthening your risk threshold, which we'll address in this book, too.) It was clear to me then that the four and a half pages I gave to this subject touched a nerve and that I'd be "tapped" again in the future to develop my ideas into a whole new book. I'm not the only one who has touched on the concept of The Tap previously; as just one example, here's an excerpt from *Hope From My Heart*, a book by a man I admire deeply, Rich DeVos:

WHEN GOD BLESSES US materially, he does so for a reason greater than merely our personal comfort. Those who have money must accept responsibility for that higher purpose. We can never escape the responsibility of God's requirement that we use our wealth in a manner consistent with our faith.

The Tap grew out of my belief in words like these, which probably have a familiar ring to you if you've ever belonged to any of the great faith traditions, whether Christian, Jewish, Hindu, Muslim, Buddhist, or any other practice that upholds service as a pathway to God and responsible stewardship as a vital spiritual discipline. Yet I need to ask: *Have you really put Luke's passage or Rich's words to use yet?* I wrote this book for anyone who is feeling that sense of longing for more and who has yet to fully embrace the idea that the rewards of success aren't meant for them alone, regardless of whether those rewards are already in hand or coming soon. I wrote it with the promise that those rewards *will* come with astonishing speed and size to those who act on the greater responsibility that comes with greater resources.

Be careful not to reduce what you're reading here into polite sayings like "be nice" or "help others and you help yourself." That's good advice, but let's go much deeper than that. I discovered the pitfalls of trying to squeeze the big idea of *The Tap* into just a few words when I was struggling with writing a subtitle for this book. If you turn to the front cover, you'll notice there isn't one, mainly because everything I came up with fell short of delivering the whole concept.

Feel It, Follow It, Find Your Calling: No, not enough oomph. I wanted it to be more in your face, more powerful.

What to Do When God Gives You the Finger: I liked the double meaning—that sometimes you feel as if God's not going to come through for you and also that you are touched, usually in those desperate moments—but I was worried people would get the wrong idea. (Made my publicist laugh, though.)

Your Prayers Are Answered! How to Sensitize Yourself to Feel and Then Act on Life's Tap Moments, Embracing the Rewards and Responsibilities of a Blessed Life was just too long, although it definitely told more of the story.

And so it went, until I decided that I didn't have to jam this square peg into a round hole. Actually, this was my first instinct anyway: Let *The Tap* stand on its own; let you find the depth and meaning and message inside the book instead of crammed into a one-liner on the front.

In the pages that follow, you'll be privy to the information, ammunition, inspiration, and exhilaration I've gained from learning to feel The Tap and then act on it. I'll share with you countless Tap-Moment stories of others who have done the same in big, splashy ways and through small, equally meaningful measures. (You'll learn how you can share your own Tap Moments at The-Tap.com.) I'll also share with you why, although I still love my profession and have a passion for creating opulent homes for the ultra-rich, my true enrichment comes from our nonprofit work through the Caring House Project Foundation, which provides a self-sustaining existence and shelter for the world's most desperately poor and homeless. You'll learn where it all started, with one of my most memorable Tap Moments ever. In the beginning, I served meals out of a beat-up old van to families who were living under a bridge not far from my home.

You'll probably recognize yourself in the stories of other people's lives, and you may even realize that you've been tapped numerous times without knowing it! This book will help you sensitize yourself so that these incredible Tap Moments don't ever pass you by again. It will show you how to tell when you're being tested, reveal the times when you should be most alert for The Tap, and help you heed the call before you have to be slapped upside the head to pay attention to it.

As you begin this book, realize that once you've become aware of this powerful force, your life can change instantly and for the better. I'm not saying it's magic or another form of the new "cushion capitalism" that's often promoted these days. (As in: Just cross your legs and sit on a little pillow, get your mindset right, pray, and a BMW will fall down your chimney.) What I am saying is that when you're ready to get up off the floor and start walking, when you're ready to take action on someone else's behalf, you will see the benefits in your own life, too, and today, not years from now. You won't necessarily get rich quick, but you will feel enriched almost immediately.

In these pages, we'll be touching on some of the puzzling paradoxes that this "business of life" presents, and also reaching into some of the more inspiring aspects of business life itself, especially in relation to the current wave of social entrepreneurism and compassionate capitalism. We'll address the unexpected consequences of the rapid ascent that usually accompanies The Tap, and this book will arm you with essential insights about how to deal with the unique pressures and pitfalls that are part of leading a tapped life—though always infinitely better than leading a trapped life.

Take it slowly. I suggest you read no more than one section at a time—better yet, take it a chapter at a time, and then put the book down, go out, and act on "Your Tap Moments," included in all but the last chapter. Share your reactions and plans with a loved one. You'll probably find it helpful to have your favorite Bible or other spiritual text handy, as you may feel compelled to do some supplementary reading.

My greatest intention is that this book will act as a conduit for your own Tap Moments, that it will open you up to the possibilities, the stewardship, and responsibilities that may have eluded you until now. So get ready . . . prepare to feel The Tap.

Part One

Feel The Tap

As an adult, I'm fortunate to be living out a childhood fantasy by following in one of my hero's tracks. Like a modern-day Robin Hood, I get to *sell* to the rich so I can give to the poor. (Unlike the Prince of Thieves, I don't rob anyone—except that when we charge $2,500 a square foot, some people might be inclined to say we do "steal" from the rich.) Through the Caring House Project Foundation, we use the proceeds from what I do for a living to provide housing for those most in need around the world. It's a unique nexus between my professional calling—creating art in the form of the most magnificent oceanfront estate homes in the world, located in Palm Beach, one of the most desirable regions on the planet—and my spiritual calling to provide much-needed shelter for people in some of the least developed and most economically distressed parts of the world. Working at both ends of the spectrum has, you could say, earned me a Ph.D. in "paradoxicology."

The purpose for which I've been tapped may sound extreme to you, or even somewhat unreal. Possibly out of reach. But keep an open mind about how you, too, may feel The Tap. Not everyone is tapped in the same way, and your Tap Moments will probably call you to something radically different from what I've been inspired to do. You'll see what I mean when you read the story of Julio Diaz who, when a mugger tried to take his money, not only gave away his wallet but insisted the robber take his coat, too. You'll see that sometimes a Tap Moment can start with an act as simple as rolling over in the morning and not hitting the snooze button, but instead getting up and doing something constructive with those minutes you'd ordinarily waste during your early morning.

As you begin this book, I invite you to look for and look forward to your Tap Moments even before you fully understand what they are. This isn't an intellectual exercise, and you don't need to fully grasp the concept before you start seeing its power to transform your life. You're encouraged to set aside any questions or skepticism for now; if you want to go back to your old way of thinking later, that's your prerogative.

Meanwhile, I can promise you something: **If you use what you read here to sensitize yourself to The Tap, it will come easily.** The touch may feel featherlight at first, like the tickle of a single hair on your shoulder or a gnat landing on your toe while you're trying to nap, but if you prepare yourself to feel it, you absolutely will. Everyone is tapped sooner or later. The question is whether you will recognize The Tap or not, and these first five chapters are designed to help you welcome each new Tap Moment like an old friend, someone you'd know anywhere.

One

TAP INTO ETERNAL SUCCESS

How much money does it take to make a person happy?

Someone asked John D. Rockefeller this question, and he replied, "Just a little more." Although Rockefeller lived more than a hundred years ago and was a man of such extreme wealth that he's often considered the richest person in history, he obviously knew something about contemporary living—and about how humanity has approached the concept of "more" since the beginning of time.

Rockefeller was also extremely generous and charitable, so let's not get the idea that he was particularly greedy or self-centered. Rockefeller was just like the rest of us: **It seems that no matter how much we have, no matter how fortunate we may feel, most everyone wants more of** *something.* It's part of our human fabric. We all pray what could be called the selfish prayer—"Oh, God, please help *me!*"—and you can know it's completely okay to do so. We want more wealth, certainly, and also more love, more satisfaction at work, more time with family or to pursue our interests, more of a sense of spiritual purpose and connection, more fun, more mental and physical health, more business, more attention, more affection, more accolades, more achievements, and, well, still more. More, more, more.

The need for more manifests at all points on the socioeconomic spectrum, and so does desperation. National Public Radio's *StoryCorps* aired a segment that beautifully illustrates my point, told by a social worker in his early thirties who lives in the Bronx. Monday to Friday, Julio Diaz said, he takes the subway, and each night on the way home, he exits one stop early to eat at his favorite diner. One evening, he got off the train and was quickly approached by a teenager wielding a knife.

Clearly, the boy was in need of more.

Knowing how these things usually end, Julio gave the mugger his wallet without protest. But as the thief hurried away, Julio called after him: "Wait! You forgot something. If you're going to be robbing people for the rest of the night, you might as well take my coat to keep you warm."

You might be wondering, *What was Julio thinking?* The thief was running away and the knife wasn't a threat anymore, so why antagonize the kid?

Or maybe you're wishing you could have reflexes like that, where a risky situation would make you bold, that you'd take a stand even when it didn't look altogether safe. Which brings us back to the same question, actually: *What was Julio thinking?*

We're lucky to have Julio's answer. He was thinking that if a kid was willing to risk his own freedom for a few bucks, then he must really need the money. The boy probably needed a whole lot more than that, too.

So as the robber took Julio's jacket and began to walk away again, Julio called out to him that there was a great diner just around the corner. Did the boy want to go there together for a meal? Remarkably, the young man paused and then agreed. Off they went to the diner, where the manager, the waiters, the dishwashers, and the busboys all knew Julio and greeted him like family.

"Do you know everyone in this place?" the boy asked.

"No, I just eat here a lot," Julio told him.

"But you're even nice to the dishwasher . . ."

"Well," Julio said, "haven't you been taught you should be nice to everybody?"

The boy said he had, but he'd rarely seen anyone actually act that way. As they ate together, Julio asked the young man what he wanted out of life. Yet the boy looked sad and couldn't answer.

When the check came, Julio pointed out the obvious: He didn't have any money, and the boy was going to have to pay for their meal out of Julio's wallet. Or the boy could return the wallet, and Julio would treat.

Without thinking long, the boy handed the billfold back. Just as quickly, Julio opened it, pulled out a twenty, and handed it to the boy, figuring it might help him.

Then Julio decided to ask for something more: the knife.

Somewhat slowly, but just as surely, the young man reluctantly handed it over.

Don't you imagine that both were gaining something far more valuable than cash and more nourishing even than the food they'd shared?
Sometimes, the "more" we think we need isn't what will truly enrich
our lives, is it? Sometimes circumstances intervene and give us something even greater.

And sometimes an ordinary person like Julio does something
extraordinary. Just what kind of miracle is that?

That, my friend, is The Tap.

Oracle of the Tree House?

Although this book is about putting your faith into action, about
looking for opportunities to share with and serve others, about heed-
ing the call when it comes, I'm not a man of the cloth. I make no claims
to being a saint, either. In my life, I've done plenty of things I'm not
proud of. And I'm not talking about the usual mischief, like telling my
mom I was at a friend's house when I was really out setting off fire-
crackers, although I did that, too.

At least once a year, I go back to Indiana to visit my family. I also
make a point of visiting the kids locked up in the juvenile detention
center in my hometown. To help them see another possible road for
themselves, I share stories from my own troubled teen years, which led
to my juvenile incarceration for stealing, selling things I shouldn't,
and constantly driving too fast, and how I turned my mother's head
of beautiful black hair prematurely white. We get gritty; I let my language regress to the way I used to talk. I point down the hall and

admit how lonely I was as a sixteen-year-old when I spent time in a cell there by myself.

I let them know that it's okay to be different. Maybe preferable. Be yourself, I say. Wear that earring. Show your tattoos. Don't compromise who you are for anyone or anything. I talk to them about how I've made all the same qualities that landed me in juvenile detention work for me as an adult: My recklessness and defiance, my risk-taking and anti-establishment/anti-authority attitudes, weren't necessarily the flawed elements; instead, the problem was how they were being used. I was just pointed in the wrong direction. Once I got myself pointed in the right direction, I explain, these traits definitely stood me in good stead in the business world. They even helped me establish my brand in the high-stakes game of ultra-expensive speculative real estate. Of course, the kids love to hear about all the big houses and rich people.

In this book, I'll be sharing with you some of the same stories that I tell them, plus a whole lot more. I'd guess that at least half of them are from my business life, since both the wins and losses have taught me a great deal, not just about commerce, but also about spiritual matters. I call myself a "compassionate capitalist," but the *compassionate* part hasn't always been there. In my early days in business, I was probably seen as ruthless, aggressive, and shrewd in a way that makes me a bit embarrassed now when I think about it. (I could have played a convincing Gordon Gekko in that classic 1980s flick, *Wall Street,* when he said, "Greed is good.") I also consider myself a "benevolent dictator," but the *benevolent* part has developed over many years of watching how

my unrelenting demands burned out the people around me and alien-
ated some who I now wish I'd continued to work with and know. So
you can expect to read about the lessons I've learned, to be encouraged
to have active faith, even proactive faith, and to learn about cultivating
the kind of creativity and flexibility that's the hallmark of every successful entrepreneur.

Hearing from someone who's been there has proven incredibly valuable in my own life. One of my favorite people to talk with is Rich
DeVos, who I mentioned in the introduction to this book. Now in his
eighties, Rich has been through the fire, too. He's one of the world's
wealthiest people, a cofounder of Amway who owns the NBA's Orlando
Magic basketball team. Before Amway, he had failed numerous times in
various business ventures, including a yacht chartering service where,
in one day, all of his boats sank and stranded him on a Caribbean island.
Once he finally returned to the mainland, he was broke, with all his
assets at the bottom of the ocean. Pretty soon thereafter, he began to sell
vitamins door-to-door, and then he decided he ought to get a few
people to help him.

Amway has since grown to become a company that grosses $6 billion
a year, and now Rich travels the world talking about free enterprise and
capitalism, sometimes in countries that don't even permit their existence. He has created millions of entrepreneurs, people who can buy
small packets of goods from Amway and build personal fortunes. The
stories are legion by now, including the one about the young woman
who started with Rich back in the day and is now a little old lady who's
worth $500 million.

Rich, at eighty-some years old, still has command over his huge empire, enjoys his luxuries, and especially enjoys the love of his children and grandchildren. The most impressive part is how he makes time for everyone around him, and not just those in his inner circle. The man is kind to every person he meets, even those he meets in passing, like the ticket taker or the bathroom attendant at an Orlando Magic basketball game. I often think that if I can make it to Rich's age in anything approaching the same psychological and spiritual shape he's in, I'll be incredibly grateful.

Much in the same way that I go to Rich for inspiration and insight, people who have heard my story, or at least seen the splash that my mega-mansions make, visit me in my tree-house office, seeking advice and an inside look at my life. We share lunch and, usually, they're curious about me and my perceived appetite for risk, and how I make it pay off. They want to see into the crystal ball as clearly as I seem to. We generally start out talking about real estate and how they can get ahead, but we always seem to make our way into the "business of life" conversation.

Some of my tree-house visitors and even a few close friends kid me by referring to these luncheons as audiences with the Oracle of the Tree House. That makes me laugh, but they're not totally off-base, at least from my guests' initial point of view. When someone arrives, there's usually some nervousness in the air, as if they've put me on a pedestal. They seem to regard me as someone who's very different from them, which may be the case, but usually not in the way they think. I don't even pretend to sit on high, and I'm pretty quick to help them know that.

They often say, "Thank you so much for your time, Frank. I know you're a busy guy."

That's a great chance for me to put them at ease by pointing out what should be a given: No one's time is any more valuable than anyone else's. Mine's no more precious than theirs.

"So let's get right to the reason you're here," I'll say.

After hundreds of visits like these, one especially stands out in my mind. I'll never forget the day when a young man drove to meet me in his Silverlake-blue Bentley convertible. Brian was in his late twenties, a real-estate wheeler-dealer and Frank-McKinney wannabe wearing a bespoke suit with a beautiful tie and his hair "just so." Obviously, he was hoping to make a good impression. He'd already made a $25,000 donation to enable the Caring House Project Foundation to build five houses in Haiti, just so we could have lunch together.

Based on what little he knew of me from my public image (the oceanfront estates, the theatrical grand unveilings, the media attention, the long hair), he probably anticipated I'd drive up in a sixteen-cylinder, eight-miles-to-the-gallon ego machine of my own. I'm sure he expected me to greet him with a flourish at the Acqua Liana estate, where we'd agreed to meet, and showcase the most opulent ecofriendly mansion ever created on spec, priced at $29 million (http://www.frank-mckinney.com/acqua_liana.aspx). Then we'd leave together and rumble along the coast to my own family's Florida castle by the sea. We'd roll through an impeccably landscaped, ornately adorned porte-cochere. No doubt he thought we'd stroll through an impressively grand front door, then be whisked away by a crisp assistant to my "tree house" (wink, wink), which would turn out to have been a euphemism for an oceanfront executive suite that would put any Fortune 500 CEO's office to shame. We'd dine on fine china, tickling the palate with gourmet cuisine and a bottle of the finest champagne, every detail attended to by a formal butler.

That's not exactly what he got . . .

I drove up to Acqua Liana in my 1988 "business-casual" Yugo (my "special-occasion" Yugo is reserved for date nights with Nilsa and driving to church on Sunday), and Brian was visibly perplexed. If he'd ever even heard of a Yugo, then he probably remembered that it's considered one of the cheapest and worst cars ever made. (An article I read recently referred to it and the Gremlin as "nerd mobiles." The one I drove that day is a much duller hue than Brian's striking Bentley, for sure, but I really like its presidential blue paint job and neatly applied red pinstriping. By the way, I'm still looking for that perfect Gremlin.) No doubt my ride made a racket on arrival, probably sounding to him like a cross between a rubber-band engine and a shaker full of paper clips. I emerged from the car in my usual attire: jeans, loafers, a pressed but untucked shirt and my favorite rocker jacket. Probably the only thing about my appearance that didn't startle my guest was that I hadn't cut my long hair.

Once we turned our attention to the estate, he seemed to relax and get more excited at the same time. We were back in familiar territory for him, something he'd expected: indulgence and supreme luxury everywhere we looked. But unless you're accustomed to seeing such opulence, it can shake you up a little. The project was and is jaw-droppingly gorgeous: Inspired by many visits to the South Pacific, the stunning estate reflects the peaceful island influences of what I refer to as "Ian" architecture (to include Balinese-ian, Tahitian, Fijian, Polynesian). Its name, *Acqua Liana,* taken from the language of the lands that influenced its design, means "water flower," and this artistry blooms between its prime Atlantic beachfront setting and the private dock for a yacht on the Intracoastal Waterway.

Acqua Liana ("Water Flower")

Acqua Liana, our ocean-to-Intracoastal estate valued at $29 million, sets the standards for environmentally responsible luxury construction.

As Brian and I walked through the home, the interior had the desired effect—dazzling—while I pointed out the first-ever glass "water floor" and its eighteen inches of water below, flowing over a hand-painted lotus garden motif. We walked under the arched aquarium wet bar and then looked up to see the tropical fish above. I did my best Robin Leach impersonation in front of the 24-foot oceanfront sheeting water walls and the magnificent 2,180-square-foot master bedroom retreat, complete with a closet the size of most garages.

And so it went as I showed Brian what we'd created, with every possible nod to the tropics and the ultimate in luxury. All of this, plus I had the honor of reporting that it had been built and certified to the rigorous standards required for a green home (an environmentally responsible residence) as defined and mandated by the U.S. Green Building Council and the Florida Green Building Coalition.

Brian got over his uneasiness about my unexpected car and casual appearance as we toured Acqua Liana, regaining his sea legs as we went along, finding himself lulled by the tranquility of the place and quickly starting to feel at home there. But once we exited its grandeur, we had another awkward moment.

I could see the question in his mind as we stood in front of my Yugo: *Do I really have to ride in that thing?*

Noticing his discomfort, I chuckled and told him, "Why don't you just follow me to my house?"

"No." He paused, obviously strengthening his resolve. "I don't want to miss seeing some of your other properties, Mr. McKinney. I want you to point out each one of them—and here, I have the addresses."

He showed me that he was carrying a copy of my second book, *Frank McKinney's Maverick Approach,* which has pictures and some of the addresses of several of our estates along the coast. So we got into my car, and once we were on the road together, he craned his neck to see one creation after another, and he checked them off in his book as we drove by each of them. Seeing the magnificence of the estates made Brian chatty, and he seemed unfazed now by what he probably thought were my eccentricities. These tremendous properties were right in line with what he had expected from me. So when I told him my family's home was up next, he said he couldn't wait to see it. He said he'd heard that my tree house was an amazing retreat and rattled on about what he thought it might look like while we made a right onto the property. He stopped when our house came into view, and I could see he was wrestling with some private thought.

Unlike the giant residences of some of my neighbors, our place was built in the 1930s and reflects old Delray Beach, which used to be an artists', writers', and cartoonists' colony. You can probably guess that those creative types weren't usually mansion-owners, and our house originally belonged to Fontaine Fox, who drew the Toonerville Trolley comic strip (probably before your time). We've kept it pretty much as it was first designed, an old-fashioned beach house with a low-profile façade and lush but loose jungle landscaping. It sits on two and a half acres, and given its two guest houses out back, by most people's standards, it would be considered a comfortable, upscale beach home that just jumped out of a Norman Rockwell canvas.

Still, it's no Acqua Liana.

Brian was quiet as we walked to the base of the tree-house ladder. His gaze traveled up the rungs, took in the gnarled branches of the strangler fig tree that embraces the modest building, and then fell again to rest on his shoes. I looked at his highly polished Italian lace-ups, too, and asked, "Do you want to climb, or would you rather go into the house and across the suspension bridge?"

Brian decided to tackle the ladder.

Once we were in my office, which has the feeling and scale of a grown-up boy's hideaway, Brian looked around. "Up there's where I have the king-size bed and flat-screen TV for relaxing," I told him, pointing to a small loft space over my desk. "And take a look out that picture window . . . there's the view that inspires me when I'm designing our homes and writing my books."

It was a beautiful day, and the warm, yellow light glistened on the waves of the Atlantic. Brian stared out the window for a few moments. I was thinking to myself that the azure ocean was an even more brilliant color than Brian's Bentley. A cooling breeze stirred the manuscript for this very book on my desk.

"Well," he said. "It is peaceful up here."

"Not bad, right? It's just the right size for me, and I love having so many windows—there are twelve—plus all the wood." I mentioned the hardwood under our feet and the cedar on the walls, as well as my desk made of bamboo. I opened the door to the tiny bathroom, complete with a toilet, shower, and sink, and suggested that before he left for the day, he'd want to check out the porthole window in there, which was salvaged from a sunken trawler off the coast of Key West in the 1920s.

My Oceanfront Tree-house Office

My getaway, where I wrote The Tap: *The infamous Frank McKinney oceanfront tree-house office with suspension bridge in the foreground.*

"Just outside that door is the suspension bridge connecting the tree house to our master bedroom." I motioned to the right of my desk as I sat down behind it. "If you decide you want to go out that way later, you're welcome to do that."

Brian sat down on the other side of my desk, taking one of the two other chairs in the office. (At 220 square feet, including the loft, the tree house is about the same size as one of the broom closets at Acqua

Liana.) Marta, who helps run our household, brought us some Italian takeout from Rotelli's to eat, along with a couple of bottles of water, and then left us alone. Brian finally spoke his mind.

"I don't really get this, Mr. McKinney," he said. "You build these amazing homes for other people, you risk and make millions in real estate, yet you live like a regular guy. You're definitely unique, but you seem down-to-earth. You're doing well for yourself, obviously, but . . . uh, I expected your lifestyle to be more lavish."

I smiled at him and raised my eyebrows.

"Not that I'm complaining," he hurried to add. "I'm just curious."

Brian was on to something. I admitted to him that there was a time in my life when I would have been a better spokesman for extravagance. Once, I'd bought myself both the Suzuki Hayabusa and the Kawasaki ZX12, just so I could be *sure* that I owned the world's fastest production motorcycle. I'd "invested" in my share of fine motor vehicles, including several HUMMERs and a Ferrari, too, but the truth is that was a pretty long time ago. Back then, I thought I wanted to live the lifestyles of the rich and famous, but I eventually learned that material things don't imbue their owners with any personal depth—and in many cases seem to guarantee shallowness. Since then, I've done my best to outgrow all that.

My most highly revered role models all make a point of living relatively simply without flaunting the usual trappings of financial wealth, and I've used their example as my guide. Just recently, when I was on a personal retreat, I reminded myself how important this is by identifying one of my "big picture" goals for this year: *Do less to enjoy more.*

That doesn't mean I want to spend more time on my couch, but I want to continue to *simplify* so that I can focus on enjoyment more than on the stuff that might clutter up my life.

When I explained all this, Brian looked interested but unconvinced.

The time had arrived, the point I'm eager to reach during any of these tree-house lunches: the moment when I get to share my ideas about The Tap.

"Let me tell you about something that happened to me in the mid-1990s," I began, "the day after we'd set a record with a multimillion-dollar property sale."

This is the story I tell everyone who wants to know what a Tap Moment is. It's one of the most significant examples of The Tap that comes from my own life, though there have been many, many more taps since then.

On that day, our record-breaking sale was teased on the front page then carried over to page two of our local newspaper, and when I opened the paper, there I was with the house, my big grin the focal point of the photo. My fists were raised in triumph, like the bronze statue of Rocky Balboa. *Did my suit look good? Yeah, it was sharp. Was my hair right? Yes, as big as ever. How about the house in the background: Did it sparkle? Like the diamonds in my wife's earrings.*

Then the oddest thing happened. My eyes swept across the fold and there, on page three, was a man who looked so much like me that I stopped and stared at him, too. Have you ever been told you look like someone? And usually you don't think so, but then there's that rare instance when you think, *Oh, my goodness! I do look like that person!* This was like that for me: He was standing in line at a soup kitchen, home-less and hungry. He had a beard, but I tell you, it was like looking at a long-lost twin. If I didn't shave for a while, nor blow-dry my hair and change my clothes for a week, I could look like I lived under a bridge, too.

I was shifting my eyes back and forth, wanting to focus and read about myself and my landmark sale, but my gaze kept returning to the other me. I couldn't help it. I realize now that in that moment, I was given a choice: *I could turn to the back of the paper and scan the ads for some new Mercedes to buy as a reward for my big achievement, or I could raise my awareness.* I stopped and thought hard about what it meant to see my accomplishments celebrated on one page and the needs of someone else highlighted on the page directly opposite.

I paused, closed the paper for a moment, and wondered in awe, *Could there be a more obvious message? There but for the grace of God go I . . .*

It was as if God had rested his hand on my shoulder and said, "Son, pay attention." I don't believe that God edits my local paper, but I do believe that God works through other people and that other people's work is a conduit for Tap Moments. It certainly was true for me that day.

Of course, attention and awareness are just the first steps. **Next comes action.** Right then, I picked up the phone and called The Caring Kitchen, the organization featured in the story and where the man in the photo had been fed, and when I asked what I could do to help, they signed me up to serve food once a week.

So that's what I did. That's it. Served meals to the homeless once a week before *Monday Night Football.* I didn't come in like the cavalry to save anyone; I assisted in the small way that I could. Next thing I knew, I was serving food out of the soup kitchen's beat-up old van to a family that lived under a bridge less than three miles from my own home. Of course, the family appreciated what I shared with them, yet I felt that I received no less nourishment than they did. At first, it mainly helped me feel less guilty for the successes I enjoyed. But in time, it fed a growing sense of responsibility and gratitude in a way that no other activity in my life had until then.

This was the beginning of my understanding of the timeless biblical wisdom, *from those to whom much is entrusted, much will be expected.* This is when it started to seep into my brain that since I had started to reap personal rewards from my success, it was time to start sharing, even if it meant doing something as seemingly small as showing up each week to dole out spaghetti and meatballs and a cold Capri Sun.

At that time, the idea of providing housing around the world to people who are poor and homeless wasn't even on my radar. Would I ever have been inspired to take on the Caring House Project Foundation if I hadn't put in my time with the soup kitchen? Maybe not. (Certainly, the foundation might have been called something different, as the "Caring House" name pays homage to The Caring Kitchen.) For me, The Tap has had a domino effect, as if God's own finger nudged that first piece and set the whole chain of events in motion.

"Brian," I said to my guest, "you know what great things money can buy. But I'll bet you already understand that money isn't everything."

He nodded and let me continue to talk about how I think it's really important to understand what money is *not*: It's not the key to happiness, that's for sure. It certainly ensures that our most basic needs for food and shelter are met, but those things aren't the keys to happiness either, as some who live in poverty can attest. I've met people who have shown me that even when you sleep in a cardboard shack and literally eat dirt for dinner, it's still possible to have joy.

Could money provide relief, a greater level of comfort, and even greater self-confidence to people who live in those conditions? Absolutely, just as $20 gives relief and comfort to a boy so desperate he'll steal at knifepoint, just as a paycheck gives relief and comfort to anyone who earns it, just as the sale of one of my estates gives me relief, comfort, and confidence. But the money itself, whether in small sums or large, doesn't create happiness.

For that reason, I don't delude myself that by providing shelter to people who desperately need it I'm "giving" them happiness or joy. That's not the point, anyway. The point is that I have been blessed with great material resources, and sharing those resources is my responsibility—if I can provide some relief and comfort, then I will, because it's in my power to do so, and it's in line with my faith. But I can't start believing that I'm anybody's savior. It just doesn't work that way.

I joked with Brian, "I'm no angel, so it's reassuring to know that I've applied a liberal amount of WD-40 to the hinges of the Pearly Gates, you know?"

The corners of his mouth lifted, and then he leaned toward me.

"Yes," he responded. "I get it. And you're right: My money hasn't guaranteed my happiness, either. But I do love my cars, my clothes, my lifestyle. Are you telling me that I have to give up all that to be happy?"

"No, not in the least," I assured him. That's not what God wants for you, either. It's true: I'm not trying to tell anyone that they have to live exactly like me to feel fulfilled. **What I do believe is that for anyone who wants more out of life, you need to start looking for opportunities to do more for others, whether that comes in the form of sharing your gifts of time, talent, or treasure.** You need to start recognizing Tap Moments for what they are and who they are meant to benefit.

"So I have to ask you, Brian, are you looking for more out of life, too?"

Julio Diaz and I are obviously on the same wavelength, and Brian, like the teenager who was asked the same question, remained silent as he thought about his answer. Then a tear streaked his cheek, surprising both of us.

He swallowed.

I waited.

YOUR CHAPTER 1 *Tap* MOMENTS

- We all want something more, no matter how much we already have, and that is okay.

- Praying for more shows that you trust God to help you get it. It shows your faith in God.

- From those to whom much is entrusted, much will be expected. Sharing the material resources that you've been blessed to receive is a responsibility. What will you share?

- Money provides people with relief, comfort, and often confidence. It's important to understand what it doesn't provide, too: not joy, not happiness, not fulfillment. Where do you stand on this?

- If you want more out of life, start looking for opportunities to do more for others, whether you decide to share your gifts of time, talent, or treasure.

Two

DESERVE WHAT YOU ASK FOR

AT FIRST, BILLIONAIRE PHILANTHROPIST Bill Gates resisted meeting with Bono. A sit-down with the rock star and activist wouldn't be all that valuable, he thought. "World health is immensely complicated," he said, and making a difference in this complex arena was his primary focus. Glad-handing with U2's front man wasn't anywhere near the top of his priority list.

The Microsoft mogul didn't realize that Bono was just as intensely focused as he and his wife, Melinda, were, especially when it came to the relevant facts and data, metrics and statistics. When the Gateses finally consented to meet Bono, the three of them bonded immediately over their mutual love of the numbers that illustrate global poverty. They also shared a shrewd yet optimistic vision for changing the world. The enormous changes they could create by joining forces became obvious to everyone, and they quickly got to work.

It didn't take long for their relationship to bear fruit. *Time* put the trio on the cover of the magazine on December 19, 2005, calling them "The Good Samaritans" and naming Bill, Melinda, and Bono its "Persons of the Year." The cover story explained their powerhouse alliance:

LIKE MANY GREAT TEAMS, this one is more than the sum of its symbols. Apart from his music stardom, Bono is a busy capitalist (he's a named partner in a $2 billion private equity firm), moves in political circles like a very charming shark, aptly named his organization DATA (debt, AIDS, trade, Africa) to capture both the breadth of his ambitions and the depth of his research. Meanwhile, you could watch Bill and Melinda coolly calculate how many lives will be saved by each billion they spend and miss how impassioned they are about the suffering they have seen. "He's changing the world twice," says Bono of Bill. "And the second act for Bill Gates may be the one that history regards more."

I love that last line: *the second act may be the one that history regards more.* It speaks directly to The Tap and the question of wealth and its power in the hands of a responsible steward. I believe that these three people have amassed their riches and been endowed with such notoriety and staying power because of what they have done with those blessings. More to the point, God entrusts those responsible stewards, tapping them with a responsibility greater than they could imagine. Why? *Because they can and want to handle it.*

Did Bill Gates know that by inventing some software, he'd later be in a position to touch millions of lives through his foundation? Did Bono know, when he was first singing "Sunday Bloody Sunday," that he'd ever have the clout to change nations? I doubt it. Bill was just a geeky engineer, and Bono was just a punk. But God knew. God had bigger plans, and now look what they've accomplished.

Once upon a time, I was a juvenile delinquent—a trouble-making, long-haired bad boy—but God had a plan for me, and I believe God has a plan for you, too. Through free will, you have a choice about whether to fulfill that plan or not, even if you've resisted so far. Second acts and second chances aren't reserved for the wealthy and famous. In life, all of us are given a certain number of "do-overs" where we get to set aside the past and step forward into a new future. We grab that imaginary eraser, turn around to the imaginary chalkboard, and wipe the past clean to start with a clear slate. Rewriting your own personal history book is within your control. All the mistakes and poor decisions can be annihilated, obliterated, and forgotten.

Some of those do-overs are built-in, like a mulligan in golf. At life's milestones, everyone gets a fresh start: changing schools or graduating, relocating, the first job, or a marriage, for example. *I choose to make something new of myself,* you can say. *I can take on the professional challenge of an intrapreneurial approach* if you work for a company. Or *I can become an entrepreneur* if you want to pursue free enterprise on your own terms. *I don't have to be that person anymore who never thought I'd find love—or that person who finds love every other weekend. I can settle down with this person who's brought out the best in me. I want*

to make the most of the change of scenery in my life and leave behind
behavior that was inhibiting my personal growth.

Some of those opportunities for starting over aren't built in. Some
do-overs come with life's unpredictable shake-ups, times when you get
in touch with your mortality (through illness, the death of a loved one,
or near-death for yourself) or come face-to-face with the real possibilities of your own future. At age nineteen, I was actually thrown in jail,
not just juvenile detention, for some of the same stuff that had landed
me in the lower-level correctional system when I was younger: pushing
my motorcycle to the limits, zipping across railroad crossings at the last
second to beat the oncoming train, racking up speeding tickets by the
pocketful. I'd allowed my adrenaline addiction to get out of control.
But that time, I wasn't locked up with a bunch of other kids; I was in
there with veteran drug dealers, pimps, people who were strung out,
people who were so deeply into a life of crime that a few nights or
months in jail were routine.

When I walked past the guard station for intake, which is where they
check to make sure you aren't going to hang yourself with your shoe
laces or infect the other inmates with head lice, I looked up and saw
Donald Trump on the TV. Although I didn't know much about him at
the time, I said to myself, *I've got a lot more in common with that guy*
than with the people in this jail. I clearly saw my two paths and decided
right there to stop recklessly using the U.S. highway system as my personal race track, a track that would ultimately lead me to nowhere. In
the more than twenty-five years since, I've received only two traffic tickets, neither of them for anything like my old antics.

At every fork in the road, you get to pick whether you go the right way or the left. These decisions are presented to every one of us in the form of Tap Moments, offering us the opportunity to either head in the new direction God makes for us, the direction that leads us to greater things, or to stay on the road we know.

Does God Want You to Be Rich?

PASTORS, PRIESTS, RABBIS, and other religious leaders and biblical scholars are weighing in on this question, analyzing scripture and debating theology. That's fine for them to work out, but for you and me, we need to acknowledge and examine one irrefutable fact: Since you're reading this book, we can assume you're already rich in some measure.

First of all, if you compared your lifestyle to that of most of the rest of the world, you'd agree that you're living like royalty. If I brought one of the young women struggling to survive in Testasse, Haiti, to your city or town and moved her into your home, it would be like moving the average American into one of my multimillion-dollar estates: an enormous, practically incomprehensible leap in standard of living. Understand that in Haiti, 80 percent of the people live below the poverty line, their life expectancy is just shy of forty-eight years, most survive on less than two dollars a day, and 22 percent of children don't see their fifth birthdays. Also understand that poverty and its devastation aren't confined to some small corner of the world. They affect one in every two people on this planet.

- Half of humanity—nearly three billion people—lives on less than two dollars a day. A third—about two billion people—live on *less than a dollar a day*. Plenty of people in the United States, probably people you know, spend more than that just on one cup of coffee.
- As we entered the current century, nearly a billion people couldn't read or sign their names.
- Millions of women spend hours a day collecting something we tend to take for granted: water. Yet they don't usually have the luxury of clean water, so almost half of everyone in developing countries suffers from an illness caused by problems with water and sanitation.

Now, if we go a step further and redefine *riches* as more than just money—if we include not just material wealth, but love and compassion, good physical health, positive relationships with friends and family, productive work, a sense of community and purpose, and other non-monetary blessings—we can say that most everyone in the world is rich in some form.

Here's the bottom line: **If you're already rich, and I'm saying you are, I think it's safe to say that God wants it that way.** (I realize that this argument I'm making has some difficult implications, like whether God "wants" suffering and poverty, too, and I promise you we'll get to this troubling question in a later chapter.) For those who struggle with the desire for riches, it can be because they question whether having *more* than they have right now—or *more* than someone else—is good or moral or ethical or righteous. Yet here's another undeniable fact, as I've already established: *Everyone wants more of something.* So, again,

I think it's safe to say that God sanctions our desires, or they wouldn't exist in us.

Of course, there's a difference between culturally conditioned materialism, which God doesn't support, and your heart and soul's desire for more. There's a difference between a prayer that asks God for some status symbol and one that asks God to bless you with more so that you can share generously with others. It's the difference between what philosopher and Jesuit priest Anthony de Mello calls a "worldly feeling" and a "soul feeling."

Think about someone like Frederick Douglass, who I just read about again when I was helping my daughter, Laura, with her homework. He was known as one of the wisest and most courageous people in an era that desperately needed courage and wisdom, when slaves were still the abused and overburdened backbone of the South. Way ahead of his time, he was a champion of equal rights, and he ran for vice president of the United States in 1872 on the same ticket as the first female presidential candidate, Victoria Woodhull, some 136 years before there was a Hillary or a Barack.

Frederick didn't win, but that didn't keep him out of the history books.

He was hardly someone you would have expected to have risen to such a place of high honor and esteem. Born the child of an enslaved mother and an unknown white man, he was held in bondage for all of his young life. When he was twelve, he learned to read, which was illegal in those days. He was helped by his master's wife and some neighborhood kids, no doubt a Tap Moment for everyone involved. Women and children didn't have material wealth to share back then, but they had what Frederick needed most: a way to access the world's accumulated thought, especially about the institution of slavery.

At sixteen, as punishment for influencing other enslaved men and women to start thinking about liberty, Frederick's master sent him to work for a "slave breaker." The brutal beatings he endured from this new master nearly destroyed him, but in a remarkable show of courage and self-determination, Frederick fought back one day. Though slaves had no legal right to stand up for themselves, the slaveowner backed down and never beat Frederick again. (Who had the second chance in this story? Not just the hero, but the villain, too. I'm telling you, *everyone* gets a shot.)

Soon thereafter, Frederick made a couple of attempts to escape bondage and failed, but his hopes were not dead. Frederick finally escaped to freedom on his third try when he was twenty years old. Eventually, he became one of the most significant figures in the abolition of slavery in the United States. He also became one of the most eloquent speakers and influential political advocates in the history of this country. Based on his own writings and what others have recorded about him, I believe Frederick's philosophy and actions were driven not by a worldly desire for a better life only for himself, but by a soul's yearning to see equality and justice for all people. Ultimately, he helped change the nation and changed the future for a whole race of people who were once forced to live and labor in shackles.

Can we safely say that God wanted Frederick Douglass to be enriched in his character, in his intellect, in his influence, even in his bank account? Can we say that God supported this man in his desires to get more out of life? Can we say that, had he not pursued his own development—especially educationally, economically, and politically—it would have altered the course not only of his own destiny, but the destinies of men and women across the world?

Yes, we can.

I think we can accept that God wants you to be enriched, too, and it's perfectly okay for you to want that for yourself. So now we're confronted with another important question: *Why?* Obviously, I don't know the mind of God, but here's my best guess based on my own experience and observations of how the world seems to work: It's highly likely that God wants this for you because **increased riches of any kind provide you with more to share with others.**

Consider just some of the examples that I've included in this book so far: Bill Gates and Bono with their vast financial resources, Julio Diaz with his remarkable depth of compassion, and Frederick Douglass with his enormous strength of spirit. Their riches were bestowed, resulting in the betterment of humankind.

Enlarge Your Own Territory

IN *The Prayer of Jabez,* a little book about a short prayer in which you ask God to "bless me indeed, and enlarge my territory," you can read author Bruce Wilkinson's interpretation of the Bible that says God is ready and waiting to rain down good things upon us if we just ask. This is a wonderful message, full of spiritual and scripturally based encouragement, which has inspired millions of readers, including me. At the same time, I believe that the good we desire comes to us, not if we ask in a certain way, but when we act on The Tap. **Every sincere prayer, however it's conveyed, is eventually answered with a Tap Moment.** In such epiphanous moments, God calls you to do something greater, to increase your sense of responsibility in the world, to enlarge your *own* territory.

Will you act on The Tap, knowing that it may lead you to something *distinctly different* from what you originally prayed to receive? Will you share what resources you *already* have to demonstrate that you'll be a responsible steward of even greater abundance?

Your opportunities to do this will be unique to you. Keep in mind that Tap Moments don't always call you to a gargantuan effort to change the world. Some of my favorite Tap Moments happen when I'm at the 7-Eleven with my daughter and have a chance to open the door for an elderly person or carry out some ice for someone. So don't dismiss the small taps; there are no such things anyway. **The important idea to keep in mind is that a Tap Moment calls you to demonstrate two things: 1) awareness of the needs of those around you, and 2) responsible action now, not later.**

Responding to The Tap shows God that you're ready to receive and that you'll use your resources wisely and compassionately. It also shows *you* that you deserve what you've asked for, which is important to recognize so you can receive graciously. I'll warn you that it's a fine line, though, between feelings of entitlement and feelings of grateful receptiveness. ("Well, I've been good, I put in my time helping out at the homeless shelter, I'm not cheating on my wife, and I'm doing a good job raising my kids, so where's the boat I've been praying for?") Again it's the difference between a worldly feeling and a soul feeling, between wanting rewards for yourself and having the simultaneous desire to share those rewards with others.

Not long ago, I heard about Charlie "Tremendous" Jones, who has since passed, a fellow who started out as a salesman when he was just six years old, opened his first business at eight, and kept climbing from there. At thirty-seven, he "retired," having built a $100 million organization, and started two new businesses that focused on sharing his experiences and love of books. In his own book, *Life Is Tremendous,* he made my point about this trap of feeling entitled about as directly and clearly as you possibly can: **If you're giving to get, that's not really giving. That's** *trading.*

He's so right! And I say that responsible stewardship, on the other hand, is about sharing without question or expectation. It's about returning a portion of what you've been given as an act of faith rather than as a part of some kind of ledger mentality. Faithful stewardship is a *prerequisite* to receiving greater resources. You don't wait until you think you have "enough" so that you can give the "appropriate" portion back. Nor do you calculate what you want to receive and then try to give just enough to secure it. No, you give what you feel called to give, what you know you can give, as a show of conviction and confidence in God's blessings in your life.

I can offer you an example that's happening right now, just as I'm writing this chapter. Lately, I've found myself distracted and having a hard time staying focused on work because the world's poor are in the midst of a serious food crisis. The United Nations has called the problem a "silent tsunami," driving more than 100 million people deeper into poverty. Food and other raw commodity prices are rising. In Africa, Asia, Haiti, and other parts of the world where people were already barely surviving, they are now starving, desperate, rioting, dying. The prime minister of Haiti was sacked. The reports I'm getting from the aid workers we know there say that they've seen nothing like this in more than thirty years.

Tap, tap, tap.

I've had this overwhelming feeling that what we need to do is commandeer some kind of cargo plane, cut through the red tape, and get as much food on the ground as possible. The villages we're building are important, but this situation is reaching such a fever pitch that to do nothing and still call ourselves a humanitarian organization makes no sense. After all, who would really choose a better house over food for the family when you're starving? So this week I put down my pen, stopped paying daily attention to our real estate projects, and, with the agreement of the Caring House Project Foundation board and the support of donors, we've provided a million meals to the starving people of Haiti, over 250,000 pounds of food. We called it "Frank McKinney's One Million Meals Emergency Relief Effort."

Those million meals, we figured, would cost us about $100,000 to provide. So we contemplated, briefly, cutting back on the homes we'd planned for one of the villages we're working on right now in Gonaives, but we quickly dismissed that, knowing we're committed not only to helping the Haitian people through this crisis, but that it's also important to stay focused on creating self-sustaining solutions that include food and also shelter, medical services, and so on. So we decided just to hang it out there and have faith that the extra $100,000 would come in somehow. We trusted that we'd figure it out.

Mind you, as I write this book, the real estate market is in an acute depression. We just experienced the first year of nationwide property value depreciation in more than seventy-seven years, and my home state of Florida was hit three times as hard as the rest of the country. Yes, we can all say we lived through the "Great Real Estate Depression of '08." Meanwhile, our $29 million spec home, Acqua Liana, remains *unsold* and we've started another, Crystalina, a $30 million oceanfront masterpiece, again, as always, on speculation. And, when I last checked, those were leaves growing on the trees outside my office, not $100 bills. In short, things are extremely tight for me and my family, so this $100,000 commitment is no small thing for the foundation.

Two days after I promised to send the food, a check arrived in the mail for $200,000. A Tap Moment indeed.

This windfall came from a contributor we know and love, but it was completely unexpected. I'd asked for a big donation a few months ago for one of our villages, and in the past, this person has usually been kind enough to write us a check for half of whatever I ask, and to send it in midsummer. Remarkably, this time the check was for *more* than I'd asked, and it's come now, months earlier than usual. It's early for this donor but not a moment too soon for us or the people we'll feed. Right on time, I'd say.

Being of service to others helps you get over whatever guilt you might be feeling about your comfortable life; it can also help you get over the self-satisfaction associated with sharing your blessings. Personally, I guard against feeling self-congratulatory about our efforts in Haiti and rarely feel that way anymore. Yet this new situation has deepened my sense of responsibility. Life has presented another Tap Moment opportunity and made me think again that what we've been doing there has been important, crucial. The orphanages and the homes, the community centers, the clinics, the clean water, and renewable agriculture—all these elements going into the Caring House Project Foundation villages radically change people's lives. *But none of them mean anything without food.* So we're tapped again, and we do what we're called to do, at once.

It's true: Responding to The Tap tends to put everything into a new perspective. It's wonderful medicine, an elixir for the soul.

What About Brian?

THIS BRINGS US back to the visitor in my tree house, Brian, who was fighting tears after I asked him if there was something more that he wanted out of life.

When he finally spoke, he told me that he usually felt empty and lonely and a little bit bored. He was embarrassed, he said, to be crying in front of me, and he hastily wiped his face. Then he finally came out with it: "The truth is that I don't really know what I want. I used to be so hungry, so eager to get the deal, so committed to being the best at what I do. But now . . . something's missing. I just don't know . . ."

Relating this story to you now, I'm struck by the irony. It hasn't been that long since Brian sat with me in the tree house, and I can't help but pay attention to the stark contrast between his complaints and the situation in Haiti. The Haitians are literally starving, and he was whining because he'd *lost* his "hunger." They know exactly what they need more of, and Brian can't quite put his finger on why he feels so empty. There's another major difference: In a dire state of poverty, you're stripped of the luxury of self-pity. Survival becomes a much more compelling focus.

Of course, Brian's desperation felt no less real to him just because he'd heard that others face much worse conditions. If you've ever experienced any of the feelings he was expressing to me, you know that they don't feel trivial, even if—let's go on ahead and admit it—they certainly are in comparison to the crushing circumstances of at least half the people who share the planet with you. It's like that scolding parents give their children: "Finish all the food on your plate, because there are starving children in Africa." It's a laughable bit of advice, mostly because you realize how very little impact and importance the reality of others' starvation has on a child with a full belly.

But this brings us right to the heart of the problem, the main thing I wanted to convey to Brian. He said he didn't know what he wanted, yet he had just told me what it was: He was feeling empty, so he longed for more meaning. He was feeling lonely, so he longed for more companionship. He was feeling bored, so he was longing for more engagement with and excitement from his own life. Like so many people who have achieved some measure of success, he was probably unsatisfied with it. He wasn't pushing the envelope any more. He'd reached that rung on the ladder that before had seemed so far off. But the reality was slapping him in the face: the solution isn't new envelopes and new rungs. Teacher and author Eckhart Tolle once posed this apt question:

ARE YOU ALWAYS FOCUSED on becoming, achieving, and attaining, or alternatively chasing some new thrill or pleasure? Do you believe that if you acquire more things you will become more fulfilled, good enough, or psychologically complete? Are you waiting for a man or woman to give meaning to your life?

I thought about this passage, one of my favorites from Tolle's book *The Power of Now,* because it speaks so eloquently to me and many of the people I know and meet every day. Once upon a time, I had been on a constant adrenaline rush, always racing to the next extreme. (Nowadays, it's more of an adrenaline drip.) It certainly seemed to relate to Brian's situation. Even if he didn't fully understand it, his boredom probably reflected a constant pursuit of the next high, the next thrill, the next *whatever,* and an inability to rest in the moment, to appreciate what he has and can give right now. He wasn't moved by the desperate situations of others mainly because he wasn't allowing himself to pay attention to them or to see how he might play a role in alleviating someone else's difficulties. He couldn't see how this might actually be the new focus he needed to get that "something" he thought was missing in his life.

I asked his permission to comment on what I'd observed so far that day. "You know, we've spent a little bit of time together, so I wonder if it would be okay if I say a few things about what I've seen in you."

He agreed, holding his breath while he waited for my comments.

"You seem like a nice guy, Brian. You've shown some grace under pressure today. When you climbed into my Yugo, and later when you went up that ladder, I gotta say I was impressed," I teased.

Brian finally exhaled as he laughed quietly.

"Plus you obviously care about your appearance and look sharp in a suit. But I wonder if you really get how fortunate you are, what immense gifts you've been given that you could share with the world. And I'm not just talking about the money, although the donation you made to the Caring House Project Foundation is greatly appreciated. You gave that $25,000 because you wanted something more for yourself—and in the process you shared very generously with others, funding the construction of five houses. So I want to thank you again for that.

"But more important than my thanks, I hope you take away a sense of the great good you've done today. When you drove up the coast in your Bentley to see me, looking forward to this meeting and getting to tour the mansion and see the other properties, later climbing into the tree house—what you really did, by coming and sitting in that chair and eating takeout with me—was to provide shelter to five families, and that's *forty people* who were living in mud shacks and under the stairs of a church. That's what you've got to go home and think about tonight.

"Don't drive away talking on your cell phone with your friends about the mansions or laughing at my car. When you put your head on the pillow tonight, why don't you feel really great that you put forty home-less people into permanent shelter today? Please be sure to thank your-self, and then, more important, to thank God that you have the resources to do such a thing. The truth is that you've been tapped and you didn't even know it. You even *acted* on The Tap without being aware of it."

Brian's eyes were getting a little misty again, but I pressed him.

"So I encourage you to start looking for even more ways you can share—on purpose. Will it be more charitable donations, or do you have a skill you could lend to help someone? Do you have even an hour or two each week where you can be of assistance somewhere? Do you want to join a service organization, or do you want to find some other volunteer work in your community? I suggest you go do some job that anyone can do—but not just anyone *will* do."

While Brian thought for a moment, I prompted him, "I'll bet there's something, someone, or someplace in your life that you already know about that needs your help."

He picked at the knee of his trousers as he told me, "There is this one woman, a nurse, who keeps asking me to help her with a senior center in our area. She helped take care of my father before he passed away last year, and she's been bugging me to get involved, to be a member of the board and to come talk with the old folks sometimes. It sounds like a worthwhile thing, but I don't know."

"What's holding you back?" I asked.

"I don't know. I just feel like I don't have the time, and I don't know her all that well, and I don't really let new people into my life that easily. What would I have in common with those people, anyway?"

Brian's response was so familiar to me. These were the same excuses I'd heard from other people who'd sat where he was sitting. They are the same excuses that tempt me on occasion. I could have told him that he obviously had plenty of time if he was spending half a day with me, that letting a new person into his life might help with some of those lonely feelings he'd mentioned, and that there was at least one very important thing he had in common with those people: They wanted more out of life, too. I could also have pointed out that he said "I don't know" a lot whenever he was confronted with the big questions, and I was starting to get the impression that he was a chronic overthinker. But I didn't say that. Instead, I asked him a few questions.

"Okay, Brian, I understand what you're saying. But what if you decided not to let any of those things get in your way? What if you don't need to *know* for sure before you take some positive action? What if this woman is tapping you for a reason? What if you have something special that will make all the difference for 'those people'? What if 'those people' will make all the difference for you?"

I paused and then asked, "What if you're being tapped again, right now?"

Your Chapter 2 *Tap* Moments

- It's often the second (or third or fourth) act that history regards more . . . Is it time for a new act in your life?

- Riches mean nothing without enrichment in your own life.

- Faithful stewardship is a prerequisite to receiving greater resources.

- A Tap Moment calls you to demonstrate two things: 1) awareness of the needs of others, and 2) responsible action now rather than later. Where will you next show your new knowledge?

Three

It's No Secret

Yes, I've got stories of how I envisioned some great thing and then it materialized, manifested, just as I'd imagined it would. The publishing of this book. The $200,000 check I mentioned in the last chapter. The record-breaking sales prices on the magnificent homes I've created. The finish line under my feet at the Badwater Ultramarathon, a 135-mile nonstop footrace across Death Valley in the middle of summer. The looks on people's faces when they moved into the villages we've built in Haiti. **All of these things and more were once just an idea in my head, a new initiative, an aspiration.** And when I've closed the loop on each one, it's seemed truly miraculous . . . but not unexpected.

"Village of Angels"

I'm taking a walk through Ange Village ("Village of Angels"), one of the self-sustaining communities the Caring House Project Foundation has built in Haiti. In the background, you can see just a few of the two-room houses, which are brightly painted in colors that sparkle on the Haitian landscape: sky blue, pink, pistachio green.

At the same time, I recognize that the initial inspiration, like the visualizing and hoping and praying, is necessary but not sufficient. Wishful thinking is never enough. The promise of having your loftiest dreams made true for you just like that is so alluring, though, isn't it? Remember Disney's *Aladdin?* Who wouldn't love to have a fast-talking, witty blue buddy with the ability to grant you three wishes?

Except Aladdin's genie is just a fantasy, a fairy tale. Likewise, the fairly new crop of articles, books, DVDs, and TV appearances that have popped up on the "law" of attraction seem to offer assurances that we'll get everything we want if we just want it enough. That message can be fairly enticing in a make-believe, abundance-manifestation-legs-crossed-on-your-cushion-and-a-BMW-falls-down-your-chimney sort of way.

Or maybe it was just the media storm about these materials that was shallow and seductive. You've heard all the criticisms that the bestselling books and blockbuster films featuring the law of attraction are ridiculously materialistic, simplistic, unrealistic, and designed to fill the pockets of their creators. So have I, which is why, when I finally got around to watching and reading a few of them—way after most people had already done so, I'll admit—I was surprised that I liked them so much. I wasn't expecting to find anything in them that I would support, but they reflect many of the same ideas you'll read in my blog or my books. I was surprised to discover, contrary to the press they've received, most of these materials don't promise that when you think about something, it immediately materializes. That *would* be ridiculous. And frightening. (Remember in *Bruce Almighty* when Jim Carrey's character answers everyone's prayers with a quick, unconsidered yes, and the world is thrown into a mass riot?)

The law of attraction's central idea is that consciousness is a powerful metaphysical magnet. Yes, it is! When you believe in something with your whole heart and mind, the people and resources you need to make it a reality are drawn to you. **In my view, any clear identification of**

something you deeply desire is a tacit prayer made with the under-standing that it's in your power to make it happen. I especially love the often-quoted Winston Churchill remark, "You create your own universe as you go along." I can get behind that. I do get behind that. Mindset is a crucial element of bringing what you want into your life. Without a positive outlook, along with solid belief in yourself and the benefits of attaining your desires, it's incredibly difficult, if not impossible, to achieve much at all. I'm also a believer in the undeniable power of visualization for self-transformation and actualization.

Yet the implication that *all* you need to do is think a certain way—that I don't buy. Let's give the law of attraction's promoters the benefit of the doubt and assume that, in the interests of time and simplicity of message, some crucial elements got left on the cutting-room floor. The most essential ones include the necessity for:

- Taking *action,* not just thinking/visualizing
- Including *others* in your motivation, not just yourself
- Acknowledging *God's* role in the blessings you receive, not just some impersonal "universe," as if outer space has some interest or influence on your life

The absence of God in this law-of-attraction business may reflect an effort not to offend anyone who doesn't feel comfortable with the idea of a divine being or any particular name for it. Or maybe it's an effort to make all this sound scientific, just as the inclusion of some principles of quantum physics was intended to do. Or maybe *universe* is a new age euphemism for God, but I'm not altogether sure about that. Comedian Mark Day has this whole bit where he riffs on what he's learned about "The Secret Secrets," and he breaks it down like this: God determines the outcome of the Oscars, all sporting events, and *American Idol.* The universe? It's in charge of sports car acquisitions, hot boyfriends and girlfriends, and, on alternate years, the Grammys. Everything else is just a roll of the dice.

Joking aside, I don't get what a universe can do for you that you can't do for yourself. God, on the other hand, infuses people with the ability to do what seems incomprehensible—an important part of The Tap. **It's not that God just drops goodies into your life, but that faith gives you the motivation and strength to carry out greater endeavors than you ever thought you could accomplish.** What you *thought* you could do never comes close to what you're actually able to do when you're tapped.

Despite the classic book title, *Think and Grow Rich,* most people can't think their way to success. The mind is the most powerful human instrument; I don't dispute that. It can hold you back or propel you forward, but I don't believe in using only your head to get the job done. All of you must be in motion. Likewise, the common "wisdom" that you should work smarter, not harder, is misleading at best. I think most people believe this means they should stop working so hard and spend more time figuring stuff out, instead. Lounge on the beach, contemplate your navel, and good things will come to you? Hang out on your couch watching TV shows about cars, and that luxury automobile will pull up in your driveway on its own? You don't need to "deserve" what you're given; you just need to dream it up? That's what I call *entitlement economics* in its most slothful incarnation. It's cushion capitalism: "If I park myself on this little pillow and visualize new clients, I don't need to actually do excellent work, attempt to meet new people, ask for referrals . . ." Ah, what a life! We're back in fantasyland, again.

What does it mean not to work harder, anyway? Put in fewer hours? I don't think so. If you want to reduce your hours and be successful, then you have to figure out how to be more efficient, intense, and intentional in the hours you do put in—but being "smarter" doesn't necessarily equate to better use of time. Obviously, I don't get it, so here's an idea: Go and ask any successful person you know what "work smarter, not harder" means. I bet that person won't tell you that being smart makes your life easier, or that thinking about something rather than doing something about it makes you more successful, or even that passive income is the answer to all your financial aspirations, as so many blast e-mails will attest. Yes, passive income is a wonderful part of your overall financial plan, but it's not the be-all and end-all to creating a successful life.

Imagine how much farther you go when you work smarter *and* harder, if you get your head and your feet pointed in the same direction. Now we're talkin'. Now we're walkin'. That's what the cliché really means: "Walk the talk." *Don't just talk about it. Don't just think about it. Get up and do it.*

Magic, Math, and Mystery

I'D LOVE TO hear what Sir John Templeton thought about all of this. Although he was known mainly as a philanthropist (his full-time job from the early 1990s until his death in 2008), and he was quite possibly the world's greatest global stock picker of the century (that's what *Money* magazine called him), no doubt his greatest achievement, his most legendary *third* act, was in the area of how humans relate with God. That's because he put a lot of money into furthering breakthroughs and discoveries about spiritual formation.

And I do mean a *lot*: He poured close to $2 million a year into his annual Templeton Prize, the world's largest award for intellectual endeavor (even more than the Nobel Prize), given by a multifaith jury to someone who makes discoveries and breakthroughs "to expand human perceptions of divinity and to help in the acceleration of divine creativity." Sir John awarded the first prize in 1972 to Mother Teresa, and he continued to offer it year after year because, he said, we've invested millions in the scientific arena, yielding astonishing leaps forward in our understanding of the physical and material world, but we have given short shrift to the metaphysical questions about which we remain substantially ignorant. He has asked, "If even one-tenth of world research were focused on spiritual realities, could benefits be even more vast than the benefits in the latest two centuries from research in food, travel, medicine or electronics, and cosmology?"

The Bible and other sacred texts give us many clues, he says, but it is the height of arrogance to think that we've got God figured out. Which brings me to why I think he would have been an interesting person to talk with about The Tap. For a long time, Sir John had been a proponent of tithing (giving 10 percent of your earnings to charity), and he even advocated double tithing for those who can manage it, and reverse tithing (giving 90 percent) for those who are at Templeton's own extremely rare level of wealth.

Think about that for a moment: Wouldn't it be the ultimate achievement in leading a tapped life? To get to the point of being able to implement reverse tithing? To be able to, for example, earn $100 million a year, *give away $90 million to alleviate the ravages of poverty or illness for other people*—and live on the remaining $10 million? That's my idea of a personal Everest, where reaching the summit would be the most incredible Tap Moment I've ever experienced.

Sir John observed that life's greatest investment is putting some of your money back into efforts that uplift the human spirit, and that families who tithe are generally happier and more prosperous. He was regularly quoted about this, even to the point of making tithing into another kind of "secret" to success.

Just like the misunderstandings about the law of attraction, though, some misinterpret tithing, too, and cite Sir John's great wealth as an indication that tithing is some magical mathematical formula, where earnings times 10 percent equals the bribe God needs to grant you a life of enormous wealth. That's certainly a distortion, just as superstitious as the idea that if you don't put the proper amount in the plate every Sunday, someday you'll be hanging out in that hot spot way down south, a place my mom used to call "H-E-double-hockey-sticks," waiting on some creature with horns wearing a red suit and carrying a pitchfork.

Some people interpret the Bible as saying that whatever you give comes back to you ten times over. There are plenty of passages that talk about enormous returns on giving. I'll be honest with you, though: I've never witnessed or experienced a tenfold financial return. Yet I have seen six or seven. (Remember, that's not six or seven percent—it's six or seven hundred percent, six or seven times the original investment.) That kind of return has definitely come back to me when I wasn't expecting it. Here's just one example: I was asked to chair a capital campaign at our church, and the priest told me that he was looking for me to set an example for the younger people in our congregation, fire them up, inspire them, get things moving. So I made a pledge of $100,000 to kick things off, but I also took the priest aside and told him that, between him and me, I couldn't make good on it until a particular project of ours sold. This was a $40 million house we'd planned, and I hadn't even broken ground yet. I was anticipating that I'd have three or four years to get the job done and then deliver on my pledge to the church.

The priest told me that wasn't a problem. Was there anything he could do to help with the capital campaign and support my work for the church? "Pray that my property sells," I told him.

The next Sunday, he completely surprised and embarrassed me by imploring the whole congregation, "Frank and Nilsa McKinney have agreed to make a six-figure commitment, but they need their property to sell first, so let's all just bow our heads and pray right now that this happens soon." You can guess how the rest of the story goes, but it has a twist: A month later, as we were getting ready to break ground, and the concrete trucks were rolling down I-95 on their way to pour the foundation, a guy on a bike pedaled up and said he was interested in buying the property. We checked him out, and sure enough, he was qualified. Within days, we signed a contract, and the bicyclist paid a premium price, a record sale for vacant land in Palm Beach County that made headlines across the world. So the very next Sunday, the priest held up the article and announced, "Our prayers have been answered!"

How does stuff like that happen? It's miraculous, a mystery, one of the great wonders God uses to decorate our human existence. I do think I know why it happened, though: I was tapped to use that property to serve something greater than myself, and it paid off for everyone.

I'm with Sir John: There's a lot we don't know. However, what we can observe and see without question is that **something transformative happens to the individual who shares what he or she has been given, whether it's in the form of treasure (money), time, or talent.** This is why I constantly encourage people who are seeking more to examine their own hearts and see where they might be able to put this idea into action.

Do I think 10 percent's a good number to use? Sure, it's fine. It's got a long tradition and it's easy to calculate, whether you're counting dollars or minutes. Use it if you like it. But don't demean your contributions by turning them into a *trade* instead of genuine giving. Don't allow a number to dictate your choices, either restricting you and keeping your contributions small or making you feel guilty if you don't make the quota.

Despite my Catholic upbringing, I don't see a lot of value in guilt-trips, especially as it relates to monetary giving. I once heard about this Australian ethics professor and politician who says we ought to give away any money we earn in excess of $30,000 a year, because that's all anyone should need to live on in the United States. Keeping any more than that amounts to murder, he says, given what that "extra" money can do to alleviate hunger and illness for other people. I find this argument completely absurd. It's revolting and irresponsible. It's flat-out stupid and far-fetched. This discounts the possibility of investing for even greater growth, for longer-term contributions, for what I call "compassionate capitalism." (We'll cover that last one in greater detail later in this book.) There is no growth, no investment, no entrepreneurial seed. And it attempts to use guilt as a lever to separate you from your money, completely ignoring what ingenuity and responsibility and stewardship might have to say about proper management of any particular individual's finances. I should also add that I understand this philosopher doesn't follow his own advice, which makes me respect his opinion even less, if that's possible. My point is that guilt isn't the best reason to give.

So, again, I say you shouldn't allow a number to dictate your choices; don't let it be an albatross around your neck. It defeats the purpose of giving if you do it with a sense of loathing and dread. I recognize that it's not always easy to give with a glad heart. Like everyone else, I worry about sending cash out the door when things are tight. That's when I remind myself that sharing is also a part of my business plan. It's part of the fabric of who I am, what I stand for, how I operate in this world.

And not every single thing I do gets done with glee and a smile on my face, but I can always focus on how it is all part of the calling. It's part of responsible stewardship.

Gratitude for what you have and compassion for what other people need are simply more in line with what the great spiritual leaders *really* taught, regardless of how it may get distorted by their followers. **The main message, and they made no secret of this, is to share what you have, regardless of how much you possess.** Earlier in this book, I mentioned John D. Rockefeller, who was astute enough to observe that the amount of money one needs to be happy is always "just a little more." He also understood the importance of generosity and was a lifelong giver. He once remarked, "I never would have been able to tithe the first million dollars I ever made if I had not tithed my first salary, which was $1.50 per week."

That speaks to a fundamental principle of the spiritual discipline of sharing your blessings: *Start now and start small if you have to.* Don't let excuses like "I don't have time," or "I'm not rich," or "What difference am I going to make?" get in your way. If you're a busy person, carve out a couple minutes when you can talk with someone about something that's important to *them.* If your finances are tight, make a point of giving just a few dollars to someone who needs it. If you feel that you don't have any special talent, look again. Can you cook? Can you drive? Can you paint a wall? Can you hammer a nail? Can you talk? Can you handle a spoon? Can you carry a box? Can you shop? Can you walk with someone holding your arm? Can you vacuum or mop a floor? Can you play catch? Can you tie a pair of shoes? Can you read? (Obviously, you can.) These are basic skills you can offer, skills that many people and organizations need!

As you share these gifts with others, I can guarantee that you'll start to expand your sense of how much you can give. Those dollars will multiply; those minutes will turn into hours; those talents will grow. Your own time, talents, and treasures will increase to allow you to share more with others. You may recognize this promise from the Old Testament:

"Bring the whole tithe into the storehouse, that there may be food in my house. Test me in this," says the Lord Almighty, "and see if I will not throw open the floodgates of heaven and pour out so much blessing that you will not have room enough for it."

There are many passages like this in the Bible, and many more still in other sacred texts. *Zakat* (charity) is Islam's third of five pillars, detailed in the beginning of the Qur'an and translated literally as "purification" and "growth." Hindus donate *daan* (alms) to holy people and the poor, and they consider donation a religious duty. Faith, hope, and charity are the three theological virtues of the Catholic catechism. The Judeo-Christian tradition includes the 10 percent tithe (*maaser* in Hebrew). Giving whatever amount—the percentages range from unspecified (as in Buddhism) to about 20 percent (as in the Baha'i faith) and up to 90 percent (if you're in Sir John Templeton's league)—

is quite obviously part of God's plan for us, not a hidden doctrine or one limited to a particular sect or denomination. Clearly, the wisdom and benefits of sharing your blessings was never intended to be kept a "secret." No! It's intended for *all of us* so that we may live life more abundantly.

Right now, I encourage you to finish this paragraph and close this book. Seriously, just get to the end of it and then get out of here. Go pick up the phone, or walk out your door, in search of a place to share something of yourself. Come back to read the next chapter only after you can say, "I did it!" *Now, grab a snack or a soda, shut the book, and go!*

YOUR CHAPTER 3 *Tap* MOMENTS

- The right mindset is absolutely necessary but nowhere near sufficient to create your life the way you want it. The other important elements are: 1) taking action, 2) including others in your motivation, and 3) acknowledging God's role in the blessings you receive.

- Faith gives you the motivation and strength to carry out greater endeavors than you ever thought you could accomplish on your own.

- Tithing isn't a magic formula. If you want to use 10 percent as a guideline for giving, that's fine. Just don't let it limit you or push you to give out of guilt.

- Use your time, talent, and treasure to benefit others, and they will be increased so that you have even more to give. Share what you have, regardless of how much you possess.

- Don't move on to the next chapter in this book until you've found a way to share something of yourself. Seriously: Close this book now, get out there, and do it!

Four

Tap Moments: The Test, a Touch, and God's Knockout Punch

Did you do it? Did you stop and execute on the initiative at the end of Chapter 3? Yes? Good.

About now, you may be saying to yourself, *All right. I did what you asked, Frank. I went out and spent some time at the soup kitchen* (or wherever you helped out). *That was nice. It made me feel pretty good about myself. But what about The Tap? When am I going to start feeling that?* If so, guess what: You've already felt the touch without knowing it. You responded to a simple request and did something to help someone else. That's how it starts: Someone asks you for help, and you say yes. Or better yet, you recognize a need and act to fill it.

You've also passed the first test. Not that I'm God's proctor, but there's something divine at work here, putting you in front of this book, at this specific moment in your life, and then you feeling compelled to follow through on what I've asked you to do. Tests like this—circumstances that make you aware of the needs of others and give you the choice of taking action or remaining passive—come all the time, giving you the chance to show how serious a commitment you're willing to make. It's wise not to let them slip through your fingers! Really, if you're not even willing to go out and do a simple kindness for someone else, how can you expect to experience Tap Moments at all? As in all things, your intention comes first, then action, action, and more action . . . then the action becomes your reward.

If you're like me, it may take more than just one touch to get you moving. It may take a metaphysical body blow. You can think of this as the "Three Strikes and You're In" rule—or, to extend the baseball metaphor, if you don't connect after the first or second pitch, sometimes God throws the ball right at you so you can't possibly avoid it. Plunk! You may be sore and mad and limping, but at least you're moving; you're off the plate and on to first base. Although you might not realize it right away, God has done you a good turn by getting you in to play. Bringing it home, though, is still up to you.

What you'll read in this chapter should help you learn to connect the first time, or at least to take a swing. It's designed to help you learn how to feel The Tap and how to know when you're being tested. If you adopt the specific practices I've outlined for you here, I can promise you that not another Tap Moment will pass you by without you knowing it.

Start by Examining Your Own Life

FOR ALMOST TWO decades, I've relied on a weekly "priority sheet" to help me stay focused on what's most important to me, to help me evaluate my progress, and to give me a reality check when I might stray. I wrote about this in *Make It BIG!,* including examples and a template so you can create your own. (I've also included a sample of my current priority sheet in this chapter.) If you want to follow my system, great, but for our purposes here, it's important for me to emphasize that the system itself isn't really the point. Good organizers and day planners abound; the best ones get you started with a mission and vision statement then help you tie your goals to those and break them down into actionable steps. **I suggest you pick one and then work with it religiously.** What's most important is that you have some way of identifying your goals and objectives and that you then *take the time to reflect on them.*

This quiet time has become crucial to my effectiveness in business, and it's also been an important discipline for me spiritually: to dedicate some of my week to evaluating myself and my accomplishments in terms of what I think is most important in my life and to see how that stacks up against my sense of personal mission and purpose. It has caused me to shift priorities and to expand my ideas about what's important in the first place.

If you were to see my priority sheets from the late 1980s, for example, you'd be looking at a list of project addresses and everything I needed to do to get those properties ready for market and then sell them at a premium. Those were my *only* priorities: real estate project #1, real estate project #2, real estate project #3, and so on—all business, all the time. (Have you ever let something take you over like this?) It wasn't until about ten years later that I realized there could, should, and would be a lot more to my life if I set some new priorities. That's when the priority sheet began to change and feature more than just addresses.

My current categories are these: *#1 Personal Growth, #2 God's Blessings, #3 Acqua Liana/Crystalina/700* (our extraordinary green house projects), and *#4 New Books/GG/Web* (the three books I'm writing simultaneously, *The Green Giant* documentary about Acqua Liana and Crystalina, and our Frank-McKinney.com website development.

On a full-sized priority sheet, the boxes are about two inches by two inches, not a lot of writing space, because I want concise descriptions of no more than ten words in each box. The most important initiative is always in that uppermost left box, and the highest priorities for the week are all in that leftmost column. Theoretically, far-left-column items #1 to #5 are addressed before moving on to the next column, but it really doesn't ever happen that way. Mentally, though, it keeps me focused on that upper left area of the sheet. Rarely do I completely fill this sheet anymore; usually, I have initiatives in about half of the boxes. (Some years ago, I'd try to write something in every box. If you decide to use this sheet for yourself, I advise you not to get caught up in feeling as if, just because there are twenty boxes, they all have to contain *something*.) You'll notice that other contributors' names are listed at the bottom of the sheet, too, and I color-code those using a highlighter, tagging them to specific initiatives where they will be helping me close the loop.

Figure 4.1

PRIORITY SHEET

★ ★ ★ Life's Organizational Chart & Goals Agenda ★ ★ ★

Week beginning Monday, _____ and ending Sunday, _____

Initiatives I shall fulfill:

	#1 Personal Growth	#2 Sharing God's Blessings	#3 Acqua Liana/ Crystalina/700	#4 New Books/GG/ Frank-McKinney.com
Goals and Objectives:				
#1				
#2				
#3				
#4				
#5				

Other Long-term Goals to Consider:

❑ Nilsa   ❑ Lori   ❑ Kimberley/Anne   ❑ Chris

Connect to Vision and Transfer Goals to Weekly Calendar

In using the weekly priority sheet, I set both my personal and professional goals and agenda starting with Monday. Every Saturday or Sunday afternoon, I take some time for introspection, clearing my head then looking at what I'd set out for myself the prior week, seeing if I met my objectives, criticizing, rewarding, and recognizing my own action or lack thereof. I make notes on the back of the sheet, which not only helps me plan for the next week but also creates a record of my thoughts, aspirations, fears, and acknowledged blessings at that moment.

- How was this week?
- How did I approach things?
- What did I do well? ·
- What did I do wrong?
- What habits am I repeating?
- What can I learn from this?
- How can I be a better person next time?

Socrates once said that an unexamined life is not worth living. I can certainly say that by regularly examining my own life, I have made it more worthwhile. In fact, the evolution of my mission and vision, both personally and professionally, ties directly to this weekly practice and my annual retreat, when I review all fifty-two weeks' priority sheets, back to back, and let that inform my plans and priorities for the next year. I have no doubt that doing this has made me unusually sensitive to and appreciative of the blessings I've received and, even more important, of their incredible value and impact as I use them to benefit the lives of others.

How will this help *you* feel The Tap? Taking time to reflect on your desires for your life and assessing your actions toward making them real put your antennae up. It creates a kind of sensitivity and awareness that you can't possibly experience otherwise. This time for reflection widens your perspective, deepens your commitment, and even gives you the chance to go back and respond to those moments—*tap!*—when you didn't realize right away what was happening.

Have you ever been tapped without knowing it? I can almost guarantee it, as most people have. And unless you inventory your experiences— your accomplishments and your setbacks, your peaks and pitfalls and plateaus—you'll never even notice that you didn't notice. In reviewing your life, you may recast many experiences as Tap Moments, times when God has brushed your shoulder, nudged you, pointed you in a new direction, or even knocked you out. Going forward, as you pay closer attention, you can start to shorten the lag time between The Tap and your recognition of it. (Soon enough, you'll actually start anticipating it and doing a kind of "Tap Dance," but that's a topic for a later chapter.)

This kind of attention to, review of, and reflection on your experiences requires eliminating a number of distractions. When you're appraising your day or week or month or year, it certainly shouldn't be in front of a TV. It shouldn't be with ear buds poked into the sides of your head. It should be in a very, very quiet place. Otherwise, the intrusions and stimulations can distract you from your purpose and distort your perceptions.

Remember, reality isn't what's "out there"; it's what you let "in here." It's your own interpretations and reactions to the internal and external stimuli you allow into your life. Taking control of that stimuli—deciding for yourself what you see, hear, feel, and know about the world around you—makes Tap Moments all the more accessible. Sometimes you have to turn off the artificial external stimuli to tune into The Tap.

The temptation to let the world intrude on you can be great. Believe me, I understand that; it's why I'm writing this from a tree house. I also recognize the travesty in letting the noise around you dictate the way you perceive your reality. To offer an antidote, while writing what you're reading here, I'm also working on a children's book right now (*Dead Fred, Flying Lunchboxes, and the Good Luck Circle*), a young reader fantasy novel. My hope is that it begins to neutralize the poison I see most people allowing right into their living rooms. Did you know that the average family in the United States has about three television sets and 105 channels? Just from that one source, you (or your child) can pick up a ridiculous amount of mind clutter. I don't hate TV or technology, and I don't think kids have to be banned from watching or using it—I love to see what's on ESPN and CNBC, or watch *SpongeBob SquarePants* with my daughter, Laura, and I enjoy Guitar Hero as much as the next guy—but I do think that we let too much of it into our lives and our minds, and that we too often succumb to the temptation to let it grab and monopolize our attention.

Not that long ago, I was watching the news (an occupational hazard for me; if I didn't have to see it, I wouldn't), and a story aired about some third-graders who'd plotted to murder their teacher. Shocking!

If I'd been just a little bit more aware, I would have changed the channel and spared my daughter and myself the images of the handcuffs and the knives and all that. But I got sucked in. How could I not? The story was sensational, and I didn't avert my eyes—and when it was all over, I was so angry at myself, because when I saw Laura's reaction to it, I could see that it had disturbed her and melted away some of her innocence. I was frustrated with myself because I had let the noise around me intrude into my family's reality, which Nilsa and I shape and guard very carefully.

One of the interesting lessons I've learned from running extreme distances is that the more you can rely on the *natural* scenery around you for company—the mountains, the desert, your crew, the other runners—rather than distracting yourself from what you're doing by feeding artificial noise into your ears, the better. Instead of listening to someone else's disembodied, digitized voice, you make yourself listen to your own thoughts and reactions to what you see, and you pay attention to the other people who are with you in the present moment. So I always save the iPod for the last small fraction of a run, using it to provide a soundtrack and celebration as I blow through to the finish line.

Do you limit the "noise" in your life? How do you clear your mind? Do you take the time to do it regularly? Any kind of awareness-building activity that helps you embrace the now will open up your receptors to The Tap. Even if you can't achieve the meditative ideal—a mind undisturbed by thought—the desire and effort to do so is still deeply valuable. I confess that I have a difficult time completely shutting off my thoughts, and I can have an extremely short attention span. I've managed to go to nowheresville a few times when I was running—raw, emptied, tired, sleep-deprived—but I don't yet have command of the ability to just stare at the now and live utterly, totally in the moment for long, which I think few people do. Traditional meditation usually puts me to sleep, literally, so I find other ways to clear out the mind clutter, like running, or being in a quiet place, undisturbed.

That's what the tree house is for. If I want to feel The Tap when I'm working, I have to sit in a space that invites inspiration. I have to quiet down the buzz of the everyday—ignore the cell phone and e-mail, stop thinking about the minutiae of my business, set aside my preoccupations—and then the ideas will flow. Trying to force it in some other way would be counterproductive, but when I shut up the usual chatter of my mind, even for a few moments, I encourage the right thoughts, the ones that bring opportunity and ingenuity.

Making Room for a New Thought

BOB WAS A talented mathematician, a valued statistical analyst at a company that sold women's clothing and accessories, mostly by catalog. He was a whiz at creating complicated matrices of sales projections and direct response, interpreting data, and communicating the impact of specific marketing choices to management. As much as he enjoyed working the numbers, the job (in his words) *sucked,* as in sucked the life right out of him. In the decade-plus he spent behind a desk there, he found himself at a crossroads about once a year, feeling as if the right thing to do for himself would be to leave, get out of there, sayonara, adios, goodbye. Whenever he contemplated that possibility, he would be flooded with excitement and euphoria . . . and then the doubts would set in. The stability and the regular paycheck were more important than his job satisfaction, weren't they? It wasn't *that* bad, was it? As the father of three small children, he felt he owed it to his family to stay put. He'd get all his joy out of the weekends, spending time with his wife and kids and doing the things he loved to do outdoors, especially fishing and camping, anything that took him into the woods.

Then he'd return to the office on Monday, and it would be okay some of the time, and awful some of the time, and every now and then he'd feel as if someone had dialed up the suction force to *maximum,* and he'd leave work a little early, grab a fishing pole, and head out to the river for some quiet time when no one would ask him any questions or try to get him involved in office intrigue.

Bob hated that job.

He got so close to quitting a couple of times that he and his wife knew exactly how long they could afford to go without his income and what they'd have to do about insurance and so on. It would be tight, but they had a plan. They could swing it! Still, he just couldn't quit.

Then, after a few quarters of less-than-expected profits, the company downsized. Eliminated his position. Locked his computer, showed him to the door, and took his name badge and access card. At first, Bob was livid. How could they do this to him? After all he'd done for them, after all the times he'd wanted to quit and stayed, how could they repay his loyalty this way? The people they'd kept were less qualified. Didn't they know that? Was it all about brownnosing? They'd see . . . they'd suffer without him.

In time, though, he saw it as the proverbial blessing in disguise. Bob hadn't been fired; he'd been let go with a generous severance package that included several months' salary and career counseling, which meant that Bob would have access to people who could help him build a resume, to headhunters looking for qualified applicants for jobs with other companies, and to those who'd conduct practice interviews with him to get him ready for the real thing.

Meanwhile, he was surprised and moved by the instant flood of kindness from friends, family, and even colleagues he didn't know that well—people who offered to connect him with job leads and professional networks. What really caught Bob's attention was when he returned to his old office to pick up his things about a week after he was let go. He'd been dreading that day, knowing that he'd be accompanied by security, as if he were some criminal. He knew it was just company policy, but the whole thing seemed unnecessarily humiliating. When he arrived at the parking lot, a guy he knew only in passing was waiting for him.

Oh, great, Bob thought. *Here we go.*

"Hey, Bob!" Jake called out. "I thought I'd just hang out with you while you do this so it doesn't feel so weird. I figured you could use a friend today."

Huh. Whaddya know?

Bob and Jake walked together to the front desk, where one of the security guards told Jake that he'd have to leave, that Bob was to be escorted in and out of the building alone.

Jake made a face. "Look, dude," he said, "I work here. If I happen to be near Bob and Bob's desk while he's clearing it out, you can just assume I have business to take care of in that office, okay?"

The security guard shook his head and shrugged. "Suit yourself."

The three men walked into the elevator and went to Bob's old office.

While Bob boxed up his belongings and took down the pictures of his wife, kids, and fly-fishing vacations, Jake joked with him and helped him feel less awkward. When Bob was done, they went back to the front desk. Jake stood by and rolled his eyes while Bob went through a security check, and then he walked Bob out to his truck. Bob was surprised that Jake would take so much time for him, and thanked Jake for making it all go by quickly and painlessly. He said he'd like to buy Jake a beer. Jake said that wasn't necessary—but he'd love to go fishing sometime.

"Sounds good," Bob said. The two men shook hands and Bob headed home.

Experiences like this provided a powerful wake-up call for him as he became much more aware of how compassionate and generous other people could be, and—*tap!*—it made him more compassionate and generous in turn. He had a sense, now, of what it felt like to be in need. He started telling himself that while he was out of work, he was going to look for opportunities to help the other people the company had put out of their jobs. He would go beyond that, too, and see if he could find ways to pay more attention to the people around him.

It goes to show you that some of your lowest times, when you feel like you don't have much at all to offer, can be the best times to start thinking about the needs of other people. It took a serious blow to Bob's ego and lifestyle to get him to pay attention. Sometimes, this is how God works when you keep avoiding the very thing that will help you grow. Sometimes, you have to be hit by the pitch. Sometimes, it takes three strikes to get you in the game.

We're given lots of chances to make it right, do it better, do it over, get the point. You're wise not to wait. If you've made the same mistake a couple of times—not following your gut, sticking with something you hate, resisting what is obviously the best course for you—you can decide right now: *Okay, I won't swim against the current that is flowing against me right now. It's time to go in a new direction.* Don't wait until you get the knock over the head that says, "Sorry, you don't have a choice anymore."

How did it turn out for Bob? He availed himself of all the services that were offered as part of his severance package. He crafted a new resume; he attended the career counseling sessions; he talked to the headhunters. He submitted applications, and he attended interviews. As a result of his efforts, just a few months after the company shake-up, he went to work as an appraiser for the county where he lives, which is largely farmland and forest. Last I heard, he spends three out of five days outdoors. He gets to wear hiking boots to work and usually takes his lunch under a giant evergreen King Pine. He earns less than he used to (good thing the family knew how to tighten its belt), but he's been fast-tracked for a supervisory position.

Bob's grateful for that, although he probably won't take a promotion if it means he has to ride a desk every day again. He's become much more aware that the job and the paycheck aren't the be-all and the end-all—maybe this one will turn out great, or maybe he won't love this one either. Who knows? What's more important is that he's noticed not only how much more content he is but also how much this has affected his wife and children. He can see now how *not* hating his job has changed the way he relates with them. He has more time at home, and he doesn't feel so caged whenever he's indoors.

Meanwhile, he's still looking for ways to help other people. He got his happy ending, so now he's looking to see how he can make it happy for others, too. After he picked up the habit while he was unemployed, he just couldn't shake it. He didn't want to. Bob has turned into what he used to call a "do-gooder," someone who goes out of his way to take care of the people around him. He and Jake do plenty of fishing, but they also work together on Habitat for Humanity projects. He likes to say, "I changed a lot more than my job."

Bob lived through the test and realized he was tapped. You might wonder why God would "test" any of us, though. Why put us through that? Doesn't God know everything already, including our abilities? Again, I don't pretend to know all God's motives, but I can tell you what I have learned from these tests in my own life: We learn absolutely nothing without them. We grow not one iota without strain or stress. So a test is clearly for your benefit, and I also firmly believe that it's a way for God to check to see if you're up to the great tasks and blessings in store for you. These tests give you opportunities to prove to yourself and God that you're worthy of receiving.

Going back to language from *The Prayer of Jabez,* what size territory will you be able to handle? Of course, certain people can manage more than others; there are some folks who go straight from kindergarten to second or third grade. They take a shorter time to prove themselves and seem especially well-equipped to handle the stresses and strains. The rest of us—I put myself in this class—take baby steps when it comes to being tested and, eventually, actually are grateful for the pressure: "Thank you, God, for putting that in front of me. I'm ready to handle it."

It can take a long time to reach that point, and even after you do, there can still be moments of weakness when you raise the white flag and plead, "Dear God, please! I can't take any more." But then you may gather your strength again and say, "I really want to use everything that You've taught me, everything I've been through before, to handle this one, too, and not melt or crumble but confront this in a humble way to honor You and the gifts I've been given."

Some of the greatest Tap Moments come during times when you're being tested. Think again about the young men from the first chapter, one wielding a knife and the other at its point—who was tested? Who was tapped? I say both were. What about Bob? Wasn't that both a test and a tap? Think about the last time you felt you were in the valley, when you were down, when things seemed frustrating and hard, frightening, or desperate. Was there a Tap Moment in the midst of that? (If you can't see it right away, think more deeply; I'm sure you'll remember something.) Were you prepared to act on The Tap, or did you brush it off?

The tests don't stop when you reach a certain level of success; affluence and achievement don't give anyone a free pass. A few years ago, I was building a $30 million mansion, the most expensive spec home in the world at the time, with seventy-two rooms, thirty thousand square feet on three-and-a-half oceanfront acres. Our marketing and promotion efforts were generating serious buzz, and at one point it actually started to rattle me, because a *USA Today* article about the house quoted a Massachusetts Institute of Technology (MIT) professor who said, essentially, that we couldn't sell it. He said there was no market for a house of that price and added that he thought I'd crash and burn, based on his extensive research. I'd be dumpster-diving in two years, he predicted.

I'll be honest with you: That freaked me out. Most people find it hard to dismiss what MIT researchers have to say, and I was no exception. I started fearing that this project would never sell.

There I was, on the cover of *USA Today,* wearing a loin cloth and a red velour king's robe with a huge, white, fluffy collar: "The King of Ready-Made Dream Homes." When I looked at myself grinning back at me from the page, then read the professor's comments, I felt my hopes fall and wondered, *Is this what my life's going to be about? Big mansions that don't sell and me in crazy costumes?* It threw me into a tailspin—one minute I was strong, deflecting the negative comments, and feeling a fierce pride in my brand—the next I was sunk into overwhelming self-doubt. These two feelings stayed with me for weeks.

Not long after that article appeared, an "invitation" landed on my desk. On the front was a picture of a grandiose estate—my mansion!—with the caption, "We invite you to see the world's most expensive spec home . . ." And when I turned the card over, it said, ". . . and the least expensive." There was a picture of a $2,000 house of plywood, built in

Honduras. There was also the phone number for the woman who had sent this to me.

Understand that I don't receive much mail. Everything's screened so that I never see junk or bills or unsolicited materials. Somehow this had gotten through the gauntlet, though. I set it aside as I read the few letters that had come the same day, and I won't say that it was glowing, but there was something special about that piece of paper, as if there was some kind of charge on it that was greater than anything else on my desk.

I picked up the phone and called the woman, who worked with Food for the Poor, and asked her to explain to me how she'd come up with this idea and what she had in mind. She'd taken the photo from my website for the mock-up of the invitation, she said. She proposed that we have a party at the mansion to promote her cause, that we use this high-dollar spec home to help raise money to build some $2,000 homes. We talked about it, and I let her know that I couldn't do exactly what she'd asked—her event would be ruined if the house sold before her date—but that I could host an event at my own home. She agreed, and that was the beginning of our relationship with this wonderful organization, which the Caring House Project Foundation still benefits.

It would have been easy for me to overlook this piece of mail, push it aside as an intrusion, rationalize that this was a bad time for me to be focusing on anything but selling that estate. I could have just said no, not now. Yet there was something about it, some intuition I had, that helped me say yes. We raised $20,000 one cold January night, and were able to build ten tiny wooden homes in Honduras as a result of the event.

One more thing that came out of this, which you might have put together already: We started investigating what we could do overseas. Until that time, we had been working domestically, assisting with providing shelter strictly for people who were homeless in the United States. Our efforts with Food for the Poor opened my eyes to the whole world. It set us on the road to using our big homes to help us build so many of the little concrete homes in Haiti and elsewhere.

Out of this test—a time of self-doubt and questioning and then deciding to see my professional achievements through this woman's eyes and just roll with it—came one of the greatest taps in my life, inspiring me to dig deeper to serve people at the two extremes of wealth and poverty.

Oh, that $30 million mansion I was so worried about moving? Sold at full price and in a remarkably short period of just 122 days.

Build Tap Momentum

ONE OF THE quagmires stirred up by any personal-responsibility philosophy revolves around the question of just how much of our lives we "cause." If we say some of us are rewarded for sharing our gifts, for example, are those living in poverty being punished somehow? Are they condemning themselves to hunger and no shelter and little, if any, education by having the "wrong" mindset or being "stingy" with what they have or doing something else that offends God and keeps them from having more?

Since I've spent plenty of time with people who seem to have everything, and precious time with people who seem to have nothing, I can say unequivocally that it's not that simple. Are there some conditions in life that are self-created and perpetuated by beliefs and actions rather than circumstance? Yes, absolutely. Are there also some conditions that seem to have nothing at all to do with the person who experiences them? I think that could be more the case for those in poverty. What I can tell you is that being in the position to help someone provides powerful spiritual lessons and growth. Does being in the position to *need help* do the same? I believe it does. Can I tell you what the spiritual lessons and growth might be for someone who lives in squalor? Given my circumstances and life experiences, I wouldn't presume.

The Bible gives us something to think about when considering if assigning blame is even a valid topic of conversation when it comes to extreme hardships. In the gospel of John, you can read a story of the disciples asking Jesus about a man who was born blind: Who had sinned, the parents or the child, to cause this to happen? Jesus's reply is instructive: "Neither this man nor his parents sinned," said Jesus, "but this happened so that the work of God might be displayed in his life. As long as it is day, we must do the work of him who sent me."

In other words, the circumstances aren't punishment for anyone. No "fault" rests with the man or his family; the purpose of this situation is to provide the chance for a miracle, the demonstration of God's love through healing.

What if you began to view every situation that seemed difficult or impossible as an opportunity for a miracle? Not that you'll be in a position to perform the miracle yourself every time, but *sometimes you will be*. Sometimes, you'll see how you can make a difference for even one person, and you can look on that as an enormous opportunity for you. You can't possibly know the whole story and scope and spiritual possibilities in someone else's life; I suggest you don't focus on that. Instead of asking yourself, *Why is it this way?* ask yourself, *What can I do to help?*

I believe God has a special plan for people who take care of those who need it, for those who seek out and act on Tap Moments. I also believe that everyone has the potential to be special and to be tapped for special things, but the question is whether you will do the work necessary to be tapped, to be special. Will you exercise your free will and do what you're reading about in this book?

At whatever level you're succeeding, for whatever amount you've been given, you're called to make the most of it and to share it with other people. When we're in Haiti after a village dedication, I make a point of talking about this with the people gathered there, from the donors who usually travel with us so we can show them the lifesaving impact their donations are making to the people who are moving into the new homes. I express my love of the natural beauty of the Haitian country, as well as for the people's spirit and joy and incredible work ethic that's born out of a lifetime focused on survival. Then I make it clear that those of us who have invested in creating the village take no credit whatsoever for what stands before us in that moment. God has tapped me to facilitate the creation of the village, and God is tapping the people of the village to take care of one another. I implore them to keep the Tap Momentum going: "How can you perpetuate this blessing with your neighbors?"

They may not need to hear this kind of speech from me at all, because it's so close to who they are already; it just reinforces what they may be feeling in the moment. I'll never forget Fekia Telus, who had been in a desperate situation (homeless, jobless, near divorce, starving) when we first met him. When we came back a year later to check on the village, we found that he'd taken The Tap to heart. He'd received a new home, which set off a whole string of life improvements for him. He'd become a breadwinner, put his marriage back together, and determined he would start sharing his blessings in the community that had blessed him. He now spends much of his spare time teaching the children in his area who can't go to school. His whole demeanor has changed: He stands taller, he's healthier, his smile beams, and all of his body language speaks one word, *hope*.

Your Chapter 4 *Tap* Moments

- Do you already have a system in place to help you regularly review your life? If not, choose one, even if it's as simple as keeping handwritten notes on scrap paper.

- Sometimes you have to turn off the artificial external stimulus to tune into The Tap. Is there something that's causing interference with your tap reception right now? Can you eliminate it?

- Instead of asking, *Why is it this way?* Ask, *What can I do to help?*

- Think of a time when you experienced "three strikes" and thought you were out, yet you were actually just getting in the game.

Five

GET OFF YOUR KNEES AND START WALKING

A GROUP OF GUYS and I were on the team plane for the Orlando Magic, a 737 flying from West Palm Beach to Orlando. No, I wasn't hanging out with the players; I was traveling with Rich DeVos and his buddies, most of whom were in their late seventies to early eighties, some of whom he'd known since kindergarten. (It's just one of the many things I admire about Rich: how he keeps friends over decades.) Despite the fact that they were all significantly older than I was, balding, and wearing suits or business casual attire while I was in my usual rocker-meets-real-estate clothes, I felt completely at home. Rich has that effect on people.

Still, not long after we took off, one of the guys leaned in, tilted his head in my direction, and asked Rich, "Who's *that?*" Like most people do when they are hard of hearing, he was shouting although he thought he was being more discreet. Since no one but me could hear very well, I was the only one who noticed. So I pretended I didn't hear him and allowed the two old friends to continue their conversation uninterrupted.

"Oh, that's Frank McKinney," Rich told him, and then explained to the gent what I do for a living, emphasizing my renown for taking incredible risks in creating the most beautiful mansions in the world on spec. "Don't pay attention to his clothes or his long hair," he cautioned, waving his friend closer. Then he half-whispered, "That's just part of his *commercial*."

The man nodded seriously, as if Rich had solved some deep riddle. I covered my laughter and thought, *How like Rich, to cut right through the surface level and get to the heart of things!* I appreciate what he said: If you strip away what Rich calls my "commercial"—my appearance and even my product (the mansions)—what really sets me apart, especially in business, is my ability to embrace risk in the face of fear. If there's anything I have claimed absolute mastery over on many occasions, it's risk. That doesn't mean I've made the fear go away, or that I'm willing to risk everything for anything. It means that I understand risk at a level few people do and have learned to live with fear *every day*.

My ability to do this has been built over a long period of time; professionally, I wasn't born this way. For six years, I bought and sold first-time home-buyer foreclosure houses before I ever moved to high-end properties on the oceanfront. The first broken-down house I bought and fixed up sold for $50,000. The next jump was paying $50,000 for five burnt-out and boarded up buildings that eventually became known as the Historic Executive Suites of Delray—after I renovated them with

$250,000, which was more than I'd ever invested at one time in one project. The first time I bought an oceanfront property, I took on an even greater level of risk, and each successive purchase after that has ratcheted up the risk yet again. My ability to handle the pressures I do now was built on that first purchase, and I don't pretend in any way that I could successfully risk what I do today if I hadn't experienced and learned from what could be perceived as much less risky deals in the past. Which one do you imagine inspired greater fear for me: my first $36,000 investment in a foreclosure house, or the tens of millions I put into an oceanfront creation today? I can assure you that first one was the hardest.

Likewise, my responses to Tap Moments have increased incrementally. As you know, I started out delivering meals from the back of a van. (Incidentally, that old Ford Econoline was so beat up and rusty that the spare tire would fall out of the bottom between stops!) My early, modest contributions laid the foundation for what we do today, and there were many steps in between: installing a mailbox for a physically handicapped man, painting a fence for a homebound woman, helping someone install new windows in place of broken ones, renovating little houses domestically and then leasing them for one dollar a month to elderly people who were homeless, taking our efforts overseas, and eventually building entire self-sufficient villages. Who knows what's next?

Risk tolerance and tap responsiveness are brother and sister, born out of opportunity and raised by consistent, conscious care.

In many ways, this chapter revolves around the central idea that you can tame your hesitation, uncertainty, lack of confidence, doubt, indecision, anxiety, or any other feeling of *fear* that's dressed up in another name. You can take action in spite of all that. You can do this by flexing your tolerance for risk like a muscle. You don't have to put millions on the line in your next business deal. You don't need to perform daredevil stunts or go 135 miles on foot in a race across the Death Valley desert and mountains. You don't have to provide housing for thousands of people. You don't have to do any of the dozens of things I do that may seem extreme to you. But you do have to learn to say yes, start, and overcome certain self-made obstacles that will get in your way. You *must* do this if you want to feel The Tap.

One of the most effective tools I offer to those people who seek my advice is a personal assessment of risk tolerance on a continuum from "phobic" to "daredevil." It was the foundation of one of the most popular chapters in my first book, *Make It BIG!* In that chapter, called "Gently Yet Often Exercise Your Risk Threshold Like a Muscle," you're invited to determine where you fall on the risk threshold continuum.

Figure 5.1

Risk Threshold Continuum

Phobic ⟵——————————⟶ *Daredevil*

If you're closer to phobic than daredevil, I say it's time to get into the risk threshold gym. Start building the muscle. Do something small for starters, then slowly increase the weight by seeking out larger opportunities with greater risk when you're ready. Keep pushing beyond your current comfort level, setting new standards for yourself, exceeding them, and then setting new ones again. This should take some time, and it should not be approached with blind haste.

Think about an area where you can do this right now: Have you been holding yourself back from accepting an invitation to speak in front of a group? Have you demurred from taking on more responsibilities at work? Have you been reluctant to join a movement you believe in? Have you still not acted on my encouragement to find a place where you can serve for even one day?

You can change all that with one decision and then act to close the loop. Notice I said one proactive act. That's all I want you to think about right now: just the one.

Decreasing your tap resistance is so similar to increasing your risk tolerance that I'm tempted to redirect you to Chapter 25 of *Make it BIG!*, because it made many of the points I'd stress to you here, and it did so exceptionally well. Risk tolerance and the risk continuum definitely have particular significance in the arena of The Tap. Certain principles especially apply:

- **To succeed in life, you must take risks.** Those who enjoy success at higher levels tend to risk more than others—and resist The Tap less.
- I'm scared all the time; I've just gotten used to it. Scared means something different to me: **a sensation resulting from the pursuit of an opportunity.**

- How do you overcome the fear that accompanies risk? It's simple:
  Start small.
- Deciding which risks to take is always a question of research and instinct.
  Do your homework to make sure the upside potential of the risk is good
  enough to make the effort worthwhile.
- Opportunities always present fear and the choice to either take the risk
  or not. Because the only way to reap reward is by saying yes, while no
  can only lead to stagnation, **the greatest risk may be in not taking
  one at all.**

In the context of The Tap, we can think about risk in two ways: 1)
acceptance of the belief that God rewards those who are responsible
stewards of their blessings and that those blessings are to be shared even
when you seem most vulnerable, even with no reward in sight, and 2)
what's necessary for you to do in overcoming whatever resistance you
may feel to acting on The Tap.

Moments of Perceived Silence

SOMETIMES, IT SEEMS as if God isn't paying attention to you. When
you have put yourself out there and begged for help with some
endeavor, when you are at your most desperate and feel as if you're
alone in this world without any spiritual support for your needs and
desires, you may very well start asking God, "Is anybody listening?"

God could ask the same thing of you. **It's in those moments of deaf-
ening solitude, when it seems as if there's no answer to prayers, that**

you need to be most attentive and proactive, not shut down and self-centered. At this time, when fear can reach its zenith, you must stay open to your upcoming Tap Moment, be waiting and watchful for an opportunity to do something for someone else.

This may sound counterintuitive, and I can assure you that the first few times you consciously choose to set aside your fear and instead be on alert for a Tap Moment, it can seem strange. But it's also liberating. You refocus. You stop dwelling on the thing that's not happening for you. You continue to act on your initiative, doing everything you know is necessary to achieve the objective, but you adjust your mindset, scanning the horizon for places to be of service, instead of worrying about whether or not you're going to get whatever it is you desire. I think of this as hearing *through* the perceived silence, instead of mistaking it for no answer (or a "no" answer).

One of the Caring House Project Foundation's champions provides us with an incredible example. I've known Doug Doebler since the early 1990s and watched his career take a meteoric rise and then seem to plummet back to earth. Through it all, he's held steadfast to his commitment to the people of Haiti—he has a lifetime of coincidences (some would call them "God-incidences") that make him believe that country is his Tap Moment vortex. It all started when he was a boy, and his aunt and uncle's church had raised funds to outfit a dental clinic in Port-au-Prince. His cousin had been hit by a car and killed when she was ten, and her parents placed a plaque over the door at the clinic to memorialize her. It was inscribed with his cousin's name and the phrase, *God is good.*

The first time I met Doug, I was delivering a keynote to a large business organization that, coincidentally, was focused on exercising one's risk threshold. Doug came up to me after my talk and mentioned that he had gone to Northwood University, a college where I sit on the Board of Governors and one of the least known but great colleges teaching the pursuit of free enterprise and capitalism in the United States. Although there were hundreds of people surrounding the autograph table, there was an aura about Doug that just seemed to cut through the crowd. We set a time the next day to meet in the lobby of the hotel to sit and talk. A few months after our initial meeting, in the spring of 2004, Doug wiped out his checking account to donate his last $20,000 to the Caring House Project Foundation, in exchange for an afternoon of personal success coaching, and we spent a twelve-hour day touring the mansions I had on the market at the time and enjoying an extended tree-house lunch together. Doug says that meeting prompted him to "think really big." Indeed, in the next two years, his business took off and he made millions, earning up to *sixty times* what he'd done in commissions in years past. He characterizes the 2005–2006 period as one of "extreme, unprecedented, and unexpected success." In 2007, he made another sizable donation to the foundation and accompanied our group to Cap-Haïtien in Haiti, where he flew over the very spot where he'd honeymooned nineteen years before (just one more of those many coincidences). After that trip, Doug was on fire, talking about Haiti with anyone who would listen, raising awareness about the conditions there, regularly and pointedly saying what a difference even a small contribution could make for the Haitian people.

Later that same year, the preconstruction condo market started to falter. The bubble seemed to burst. This meant that all of Doug's deals went south, buyers were losing big money, and Doug foresaw major lawsuits. Although he wasn't legally liable, that probably wouldn't keep some very angry and disappointed investors from trying to recoup their losses from him. In the ensuing months, he experienced a complete reversal of fortune. By January of 2008, Doug had gone a year with very little income, yet he felt so strongly about the impact he was making in Haiti that he borrowed $5,000 to make the donation required to build an entire home there, and then he traveled with us in February of that year. (During this time of nearly no income, by the way, Doug kept talking about Haiti, and I'm sure he influenced many donors to support our efforts there, although there's no way to know exactly how much money he caused to be sent our way. I do know of at least one businessman, Jim Whelan, who sat with Doug on an airplane, asked him for the name of our organization, and penned a $10,000 check on the spot. Jim is one of our largest benefactors today.)

When we returned home, Doug couldn't wait to once again share his experiences with anyone who would listen. In March, we were planning another trip for June, and he borrowed another $5,000, this time from himself, by spreading his donation over three credit cards so he could go with us, although his business bank accounts were, in his words, "pretty thin."

Just before we left for the June trip, Doug went to dinner with a developer he'd done business with in the past. In fact, the fellow had owed Doug $250,000 for more than a year, and Doug expected that debt would never be paid. In fact, he anticipated that they were going to ask Doug to return some of the commissions they had paid previously. The market was baaaad, and no one was honoring old debts. Yet, somewhere between the salad and the dessert—tap!—the developer handed Doug a check for the full amount. Where did that come from?!

Restate the Question

WHO KNOWS WHERE the rest of Doug's story will go? Maybe he's at the beginning of another financial rise or, possibly, God has other plans for him. Tap Moments occur for reasons that are often beyond our comprehension, frequently contrary to our idea of what should or shouldn't happen in our lives, creating unexpected blessings.

Every now and then, they also present inconvenient twists and turns, redirecting our focus to something more important—at least for now. Whenever this is happening, you're wise to guard against interpreting it as a "no" or no answer at all. There've been many times when I have persisted in a certain direction, and it just hasn't turned out the way I'd hoped. Occasionally, it's seemed as if I've been abandoned in a kind of desert of the soul, yet *that's an illusion*. **The truth is that these periods are often vital gifts of time for reflection, providing a chance to revise the question, rethink the objective, restate the intention.**

Most recently, I've been completely gripped by the idea of designing, creating, then selling an estate worth a minimum of $135 million, inspired by Italian and Mediterranean architecture and planned for

67,672 square feet—The Manalapan Residence (http://www.frank-mckinney.com/estate_for_sale_manalapan_residence.aspx) would be an enormous place with a record-breaking price tag. In putting together a design and consultant team of more than twenty people, and getting the building permitted (four different permits from four governmental agencies, federal, state, county, and municipal—lots of red tape), I had to jump through major hoops, all of which took about a year. After that year, I had done it: designed and fully permitted the most beautiful megamansion in the world, complete with fourteen bedrooms, twenty-four bathrooms, an eighteen-car garage, a 6,140-square-foot master bedroom suite (three times the size of the average home), lavish Grand Rotunda room, dual water walls, aquarium ceilings and walls, movie theatre, casino and club room with stunning aquarium wet bar, his and her offices, ten wet bars, two wine rooms (one for red, one for white), gymnasium with beauty salon, two swimming pools (classical lap and grotto waterfall/waterslide), shark tank, two elevators, bowling alley, tennis court with pavilion, archery range, quarter-mile jogging/go-cart track, butterfly gardens, Italian and Floridian gardens, sculpture gardens, citrus orchard, guest house, staff house, and, well, I could go on and on . . .

After all that, when I went to the bank to close on the financing that I thought I had in place, the response was not at all what I'd expected: "Given the current state of the market, we would like you to build and sell two smaller $30–40 million homes prior to the funding of this loan." *Wait a minute,* I was thinking. *I'm Frank McKinney, the real estate rock czar. My crystal ball is never wrong and all my projects turn to gold, so how can this be?* I was under the assumption that financing for this project was a done deal and had fully expected to get the money, based on my relationship with the bank and my impeccable credit history with them. But they said they wouldn't do it at this time.

Figuratively, I was standing there with the shovel in the ground—and when I was denied, it was as if they'd pulled the dirt right out from under me. I knew I could create this masterpiece, and I knew I could sell it, and as willing as I am to take big risks, I never do it foolishly. I knew I could make it happen, so I was completely convinced that the bank was denying me for no good reason. This was supposed to have been my crescendo. *Why was this occurring? God, I need your help! Hello? Are you listening?* It took me a cooling-off period and some deep reflection to finally come to accept that maybe it wasn't the right time to break ground on that particular project. In looking back, I think God was saying to me, "Slow down, young fellow. You're going a little too fast here. We're going to put the brakes on, and it isn't going to happen now."

At the time, I had to swallow my pride and agree to design and create two new estate homes, one we'd named *Acqua Liana* and the other *Crystalina*. And then—*tap!*—I decided to create two homes that would set the standard for environmentally responsible, luxury construction practices. It was time to innovate and make a market again, to do what nobody else had thought of doing. I was given the chance to rephrase the request from "please help me to get this project financed so I can break into the nine-figure price bracket" to "please help Acqua Liana and Crystalina set the standard for sustainable luxury construction. Help me be the new 'Green Giant.'" I can now see that the first question may have been driven by ego and a strong conviction that I could carry out the initiative, while the second reflected a higher level of social consciousness and will also help me further solidify the Frank McKinney brand.

Crystalina ("Crystal-clear Views")

Crystalina, an ocean-to-Intracoastal estate valued at $30 million, raises the bar even higher for environmentally responsible luxury construction.

A close friend shared with me that this same principle of "rephrasing the question" was at work in her personal life when her mother was dying of complications of cancer. She told me how, when she first learned that her mother's illness had advanced to this stage, she had felt so helpless, sick to her stomach, and inconsolable. In this state, she wanted to ask God to "fix" it, to take away the cancer, to restore her mother's health. Understandably, she didn't want her mother to die.

When she arrived at her mother's hospital bedside, her distress escalated to the point where she not only felt helpless but useless. *How can I be of any support to my mother like this?* She was dizzy, disoriented, running to the bathroom every ten minutes. She called her pastor from the hospital's chapel. "Help me!" she whimpered into the phone. "I can't be like this right now. My mother and father need me!" Together, my friend and her pastor prayed for strength of body and mind, for clarity of thought, for compassion and wisdom to help her family get through this difficult time. Eventually, she began to feel the nausea lifting, and she was able to return to help make some tough decisions about her mother's care.

She says she thinks this prayer was answered because it was focused on something other than her own pain. She also told me that this prayer, too, evolved from requests for strength to requests for peace for the whole family, to envelop her mother's transition in a sense of safety and the feeling of being deeply loved. In the couple of weeks before her mother died, she began offering prayers of gratitude, too. "Thank you, God, for showing me that I can do this; I can handle this. Thank you for giving me this time to care for my mother in her home, where she's less fearful and we're all better able to prepare for what you have in store. Thank you for this chance to show her my gratitude for the life she gave me. Thank you for the gift of seeing this circle complete with my own flesh and blood. Thank you, God, for your comfort and promise of enduring love."

Of course, she wept when her mother died. She still cries when she talks about it. But this doesn't change the fact that God gave her time and space to *rephrase the question,* and that doing so was one of the miraculous spiritual gifts that came through being present for her mother's passing.

When God Gives You the Finger

ALL TIMES OF perceived silence, no matter how difficult they seem, present you with the opportunity to rephrase the question, to reflect on your motives, to refine your prayers. Notice I didn't say that you should "give up" asking or that you should stop praying. Or that you should interpret the perceived silence as God giving up on you.

It's like that old joke about the flood, where a man decides not to evacuate with the rest of his neighbors and says, instead, that *the Lord will provide* for him. The waters rise, and someone motors up in a boat to rescue him as the man stands at a second-floor window in his house, but the man waves the boat on, insisting that *the Lord will provide* for him. Soon, the man is forced onto the roof, and a helicopter flies over, lowering a rescue worker on a rope to help him. But again the man refuses, saying that *the Lord will provide.*

The man drowns.

As he approaches the Pearly Gates, St. Peter's got his arms crossed and he's shaking his head. "You're early," he says.

"I don't get it!" the man replies. "I thought the Lord would provide for me!"

St. Peter sighs. "Who do you think sent your neighbors, the boat, and the helicopter?!"

We all pray the selfish prayer: "Help *me*, dear God!" And it's perfectly okay to do so. Sometimes God comes to the rescue, giving you the miraculous turnaround in health or wealth or what have you. Yet when it feels as if no help is on its way, it's time to apply the "perceived silence rule" and start looking *inside* for answers and new questions. **It's time to perform what I call a "full soul scan," a complete gut check, and see if you are persisting in a worthwhile direction, or actually resisting God's will for you.** As I described in the previous chapter, sitting down, taking time to be quiet, looking at how you expended your resources and yourself during any given week is incredibly valuable for this. Assessing the cumulative effect over a week or a month or a year can help you notice the signs and patterns (I'm not talking about superstition but rather practical indicators) that show you whether it makes sense to continue on a particular path or not.

Creative persistence is one thing, where you find new ways to meet the challenges thrown at you, refusing to roll over and instead rolling with the punches. Stubborn insistence is another, where you're demanding that God adhere to your timetable and ignoring those practical indicators that may tell you to find a new direction. For me, there are several items on my agenda that I have chalked up to "not yet": the

$135 million estate on hold until we get the right financing deal; some wholesome reality-show concepts I've pitched that have been shot down by a few producers who, in my opinion, are short-sighted; a documentary on the green houses we're building that stalled midproduction; my desire to be the thirty-eighth person in the world to finish the Badwater Ultramarathon four or more times; even my dream of becoming the U.S. ambassador to Haiti, which I've not yet actively pursued, nor do I really know how I'd do. I've surrendered all of these to God's timetable, and I have faith that these or, more likely, something better will be given to me when the time's right. *I haven't given up on these plans, though.* I still keep my antennae up in case there's a new opportunity to take a risk and see the eventual reward.

God always answers a sincere prayer. It may not happen in the way that you initially asked or as soon as you'd like, but . . . an answer always comes. The way to ensure that you recognize that answer when it arrives, and don't wind up confused and blaming God like the guy at the Pearly Gates, is to remain sensitive to The Tap. God may very well be giving you the finger, but not in the way that you might think. **God isn't abandoning you, cursing you, dismissing you; God is tapping you, calling you, prodding you to find a way to redefine what you want so that it has meaning to someone other than you alone. You *can* have more of anything you desire, as long as you find a way to make that meaningful to someone besides you,** and you stay open to unforeseen ways in which God may deliver exactly what you need, which, as I said, may not look exactly like what you've requested.

The title of this chapter, "Get Off Your Knees and Start Walking" emphasizes that you need to *say your prayers while you're in motion,* looking for opportunities to share what you already have. When the economic environment starts tap-dancing on your business, you can pray walking and consider what resources you can put back into your local community, or even someone else's business. When your love life either dries up or starts to look like a twenty-car pileup, you can pray walking and think about what will put more life and love into the world around you. When the pounds seem to cling to your frame and nothing you do will get you over the plateau, you can pray speed walking and see who could use your help with even the simplest physical tasks. When work seems hard and leisure seems like a fairy tale only other people get to live, you can pray walking and figure out how you can help someone who desperately needs a job.

Pray walking.

Dr. Richard Heinzl, the founder of the Canadian chapter of Doctors Without Borders/*Médecins Sans Frontières,* tells the story of one of his trips to South Africa at the time of the country's first free election in 1994, after the end of apartheid. On the day of the election, he had volunteered to help out at the polling place. He reports that the line was incredibly long, much longer than anyone had anticipated. Over three thousand people came from cities and remote villages to vote for the first time. Because there are many languages in South Africa that have no written representation, the government there had prepared special placards with photographs of the candidates so that those who don't read could still vote. Everyone was allowed to vote, and they were encouraged to do so.

Among those in line at Richard's polling place was a woman in her late eighties, carried by her five sons. She had crippled hands and feet and was unable to walk, so her sons brought her on a blanket, conveying her this way over many miles to reach the voting place. Her family spoke one of the beautiful clicking languages of the area, which has no written form, so they requested a placard for the old woman. When it was brought to her, she reached for it from where she lay on her blanket, and pulled the pictures close so she could be sure of who she chose. Her index finger slowly, painfully extended from her crumpled hand, and she jabbed it decisively at the photo of the candidate she'd chosen.

She affirmed her vote with one word: *Mandela.*

She wept as she handed the card back, and she began repeating a phrase in her native tongue. When someone asked for a translation, her sons said that she was telling them, "I can die now. I have voted."

Because of her persistence and her ability to overcome the fear associated with such a long journey, she had made a way out of no way. Her sons had brought her to this place to cast her ballot in her very first election in the twilight of her life, and this occasion represented not just a chance for her to do something she'd never done before, but also an enormous change for her country. When the former prisoner became president, when Mandela won the election, it was as if he stood on the wreckage of apartheid and showed that the people could rebuild.

Whatever we're given, we're called to make the most of it and to share it with other people. This woman didn't have the ability to walk. She didn't have the ability to read. There were a lot of things this woman didn't have, as she came from a place of extreme poverty. But what she did have was the ability to recognize the man whose face represented freedom to her and to point at that card and say what she wanted.

Ultimately, what this woman represents to me is that you can walk even when it seems you can't. You can take action even when it seems impossible. You can go into new situations, do what's unfamiliar or uncomfortable, and affect someone else's life for the better.

You can build your "tap muscle" while building your tolerance for risk. You can say yes to someone's simple request. You can overcome your fear and your reluctance by starting small. You can pray walking. You can focus on the benefit to someone else instead of yourself and enlarge your sense of mission and purpose in this world. You can be more than your commercial. **You can live a tapped life.**

YOUR CHAPTER 5 *Tap* MOMENTS

- You can take action in spite of your fear: Build your "tap muscle" and your risk tolerance incrementally by starting small and expanding when you're ready.

- Determine where you are on the risk continuum. Are you closer to the phobic end of the spectrum, closer to the daredevil side, or somewhere in the middle?

- Start thinking of being scared as a sensation associated with the pursuit of an opportunity.

- In moments of perceived silence, when it seems as if your prayers won't be answered, make an effort to be more attentive and proactive, not less.

- You can always rephrase the question.

- When things just don't seem to be happening for you, ask yourself, *Am I persisting in a worthwhile direction, or am I resisting God's will?*

- Pray walking: Say your prayers while you're in motion, looking for opportunities to share what you already have.

Part Two

Act on The Tap

Most of us don't generate vitamin M entirely on our own. No, most of us need to seek some of that *motivation* from an outside source. Because I live a tapped life—because my spiritual beliefs compel my practical actions—I've established certain rituals that I know will boost my vitamin M, along with my energy and sense of purpose. Every morning at 4:30, when I'm on my way to the gym or out on Ocean Boulevard running, I begin with a simple prayer:

GOOD MORNING, DEAR JESUS. Wonderful God, I pray that you continue to bless me indeed, bless me with miracles I've been praying for that you feel I'm worthy of receiving. I pray for the strength, courage, patience, and enlightenment to live my life a little more like you, the way you would be proud of, and the way I am capable of living. I pray that you continue to enlarge my territory so that I might touch as many lives as possible. I pray that your hand will be with me, for I can do nothing on my own, and in faith, keep me free from harm, pain, fear, and temptation. I pray this in your name, dear Jesus. Amen.

Then I go to the 6:45 AM mass every Sunday with my family, where my daughter, Laura, and I are ushers. I make a habit of taking personal retreats to recharge my spirit. My mantra pops up on my computer monitor whenever the screen goes dark: STRENGTH, COURAGE, PATIENCE, AND ENLIGHTENMENT. These reminders and rituals keep me going, filling up my "spiritual lunch box," feeding my soul to carry out the work I've set for myself.

Right now, I can imagine you shaking your head as you read this. *The Tap stuff is starting to get time-consuming. This guy's talking about praying every day, attending worship services once a week, taking personal retreats once a year, putting stuff on my computer, and who knows what else. When am I supposed to do all this?* Take a breath. I'm not saying you have to do exactly as I do, or do everything today. Hey, oftentimes I miss what most believe to be absolute recurring practices for me. Like you, I can't always fit everything in. Life can swing out of balance. Once I recognize it and can identify what's contributing to the imbalance, I compensate with what you'll learn in the next few chapters—whenever I can. Maybe the best path for you is to wake up and take a walk in the woods first thing in the morning and skip all the rest. But that's not for me to say; only you know what nourishment your spirit requires.

Let me caution you not to become complacent just because you've been exposed to some new ideas and possibly even taken some new actions. If you've taken the few steps I've already suggested, I can assure you that you're becoming more aware of and sensitized to The Tap. It may still feel like only a light presence, but *you know it's there.* So I have to ask you something: How many times in your life have you become educated to a new concept, but then it didn't go any farther than that? (Consciously or not, you thought, *I feel good because I've learned something new, and now I'll move on to the next thing without ever doing anything about it.*) So you put the book on the shelf. You pulled the ear buds out. You left the seminar. And then life resumed as it always had been.

I implore you not to let that happen this time. In the next five chapters, I'll be giving you multiple ways to get that vitamin M and asking you, repeatedly, to get up, quit reading, get busy, and act on your new Tap Moments. This part of *The Tap* is a lot like what happens with one of our oceanfront creations after all the deal-making and designing, permitting, and assembling a team are done. At first, everyone is buzzing with the excitement of buying the opportunity and the creative fervor of imagining the one-of-a-kind masterpiece we'll be introducing to the world. But then the real work has to get started. The glamour factor drops close to zero, and the shovel hits the sand.

This is where you start to produce results. Or not.

A more enticing metaphor might be lovemaking: Up to this point, it's all been build-up. Now it's time to get it on. The attraction and the wonder and the caressing and the discovery of foreplay is wonderful, of course. But if you go on and on with it endlessly, you can get dull, detached, tired, frustrated, and even fall asleep before . . . you get the picture. It's far more satisfying if you build to a crescendo and then do what comes naturally: Bring the act to completion—perhaps an extended one, but to completion nonetheless.

In other words, no more fooling around. No more stalling. No more using the need to know more or understand more as an excuse for inaction. If you're finding yourself deliberating about The Tap instead of just following your instincts, I suggest you direct your "research" toward the book *Blink* by Malcolm Gladwell. Pay special attention to Chapter 4's section 5, "When Less Is More," which reveals how life and death situations are sometimes handled better when you have *less* information to process. Do the choices you're making about The Tap have such high stakes? Probably not. But maybe that's all the more reason why you should just go on and follow your gut on this one.

Remember an old adage that I employ often: *It's better to regret what you've done than to regret what you haven't done.*

I'm not asking you to be someone you're not, or to do something that's completely out of character for you. In fact, I encourage you to be more of who you are—that's what Chapter 7, "Why Not Drive a Purple Yugo?" is all about. Of course, you don't want to focus on being more of who you are as a procrastinator or couch potato or any other part of you that holds you back. *The Tap* is about being more of who you are in your highest calling and your best version of yourself.

This section of the book gives you the tools you need to do that. The chapters are, for the most part, shorter, a bit less philosophical, more hands-on than what you've read so far. They're designed to encourage action, not overcontemplation. They help you move from tap to tap, doing the small things that make a difference every day. I share with you my lunch-pail approach in Chapter 8 and the microwave prayer in Chapter 9, both of which bring the beauty of simplicity to a daily practice that puts your Tap Moments front and center. The "bookends" to this section—Chapter 6, "Say Yes More Than No," and Chapter 10, "Think Fast, Act Faster"—give you two effective mottos and methods for seizing Tap Moments and responding in ways that help you do so more often and with greater joy.

Six

SAY YES MORE THAN NO

H<small>E WAS A UNIVERSITY</small> student, a sophomore studying history at a Midwestern college. He'd just dropped a few coins into the vending machine and pushed the button for a snack when the news anchor on the TV announced that Martin Luther King, Jr. had been fatally shot.

He stood there in the dormitory's common room with a bag of chips in his hand, stunned. Other students began to comment. Some said how horrible it was, some discussed it calmly, some cried, and some cheered. One said, in coarser language than I'll repeat here, that this upstart so-and-so had gotten what he deserved. The young fellow at the back of the room bristled. *Don't they know I'm right behind them? Good Lord, if they can shoot King, what could happen to me? God, help me!* He stood, rooted to the spot.

When someone finally noticed him there, the room hushed. In that moment—*tap!*—he had a flash: *The only thing I can do, because I'm completely helpless in this situation, is stand here and somehow let my presence influence people not to speak badly of this man, whom I so admired.* The young man spent much of the rest of the day wandering the campus, looking for conversations he could influence merely by standing nearby.

You could say that was a pretty small thing, to go stand somewhere. But, ultimately, was it a small thing? Maybe. Maybe it gains in stature only when you rewind to those times and consider the courage it must have taken for a young black man to approach groups of white students and remind them of their humanity. Or maybe it seems small when you think about what happened in the civil rights movement before and after that day. Or maybe you think about it the way that young man did: Although it felt insignificant, it was the one thing he could do.

Don't Dismiss the Small Tap

THINK FOR A moment: Which occasions in your life do you now recognize as having been Tap Moments—but you let them pass you by? Now that you know you will be tapped again, and you probably already have a good idea of what it feels like, you need to be prepared to act on it. It's important that you don't wait until you get a "big enough" tap before you respond—that's like second-guessing God, or else saying, "Hey, I know you're the creator of the universe and omnipotent and all that, but I really don't have time to run your errands. Can you give me something better to do?" I hope I don't need to spell out why that would be a huge mistake.

Try never to overlook the chance to say yes. If you say no, do it after some deliberation and with clear rationale. My goal is to have "yes" be the more natural response, and for "no" to take some time. So yes, I'll pick up the shirt someone knocked off the hanger at Target or Wal-Mart so that a store employee doesn't have to do it later. Yes, I'll accept the kindness of others, too, like the time my credit card wouldn't work at the 7-Eleven and someone in line behind me bailed me out with some cash. Yes, I'll turn right around and carry someone else's ice out to the car, or refer a client to a competitor, or tip the custodian in the airport terminal to express my thanks for keeping it clean.

Yes, you can leave a short thank-you note with a gratuity for house-keeping the next time you check out of a hotel room, walk to the back of the kitchen at a fast-food restaurant and tell the cook you liked how he or she prepared your meal while handing him or her a $5 bill, allow the woman with three kids to cut in front of you at the grocery store when all you have is your box of Fruity Pebbles and a can of sardines, or drop some extra change in a stranger's expired parking meter. (Quick tap for you: Before you go on, turn the nine examples above into a short list and stick it in your purse or wallet and see how long it takes you to cross them off. Share your results with me and other readers at The-Tap.com in a special blog called "Share your Tap Moments.")

Altruism doesn't come especially easily or naturally to most of us. Even if there are areas of your life where you find it normal and natural to say yes, there are probably some areas that are still outside your comfort zone. Are there calls you could take that you'd usually blow off? E-mail requests you could honor that you'd normally ignore? I'm not talking about those Nigerian fraud e-mails ("You will have millions if you help my family!") but about those things that come from people you know. "I'm running to benefit heart disease research. Will you sponsor me?" "I've been writing a blog. Can you write a complimentary review so I can get ranked a little higher?" "My friend is traveling on a mission trip to help out at a men's shelter in North Carolina. Would you make a donation?" "I'm looking for work in your area. Do you know anyone—or know anyone who might know anyone—who's hiring?"

A friend and Caring House Project Foundation board of directors' member Jim Toner related one story to me of a fifty-eight-year-old man and his wife, who had been living in their van for months. The fellow (let's call him Noah) called Jim and said that he'd heard that Jim sometimes helped veterans in trouble through his Pittsburgh-based Hope Lives Foundation. Noah wasn't asking for money; he was looking for work. He'd been a contractor and a good one, but because he had no permanent address, no one would hire him. Jim said sure, he thought he knew someone in Ohio he could contact—that's where Noah and his wife were parked for the moment—and said he'd call Noah back after he knew something.

The Ohio connection panned out: Jim's contact was working on six properties and needed help, so Jim called Noah back, gave him the Ohio man's number, and then thought, *I hope he follows through.* Not an hour later, Noah was on the phone again to Jim.

He wanted to express how grateful he was for what Jim had done. He said that for the last six months he had contacted every aid agency he could think of, and no one would help him. Through tears, he told Jim that he was the only one who'd taken the time to try and help and treated him like a human being. Jim asked him to be sure to return the favor for someone else some day. At the end of the call, Noah said thank you again. "God will bless you," he promised. Then he hung up.

In correspondence Jim sent me, he wrote, "Frank, it took only five minutes of my time to make a major impact on this guy's life. It's not always about the money, and what may seem small and insignificant to us may be life-changing for someone else."

Opportunities like this probably present themselves to you all the time, particularly if you're in business and dealing with customers or clients. In the book *The Go-Giver* by Bob Burg and John David Mann, things don't really turn around for the hero of the story, Joe, until he refers an important account to the competition. He knows they're in a better position to do what this particular client wants done, and he has to overcome a lot of personal resistance, but when he finally does this selfless act of service, he feels wonderful—fearful about his prospects and his career, but wonderful nonetheless. I'm not going to spoil the end by telling you how it turns out, but I'll reveal that this is ultimately, though not explicitly, a fable about The Tap.

There are no scorecards in the sky, no little cherubs marking down whether the person you helped was in direst need or could just use a little help. It's not like it's worth more points to help the hungry person than to help your brother-in-law get a better blog rating or to help your customer get exactly what he or she is looking for from someone else. It's common to think that the time you spend in the soup kitchen is much more valuable and important than, say, wiping up a soap spill in a public restroom, as if there are some giant scales of justice measuring good deeds. But there are no such scales.

This is a very important point to ponder. Every Tap Moment is meaningful, and each time you say yes, you diminish your reluctance to respond the next time someone's need is presented to you. I don't know that the reluctance ever disappears completely, but it definitely dwindles. You don't stop being discerning, avoiding things that are obviously bogus requests or blatant scams, but you can stop scrutinizing and holding on with such a tight fist to every minute, every penny, every bit of advice or encouragement you might be able to give.

In God's eyes, I'm sure, every act of generosity, kindness, and compassion is equally valued. Yet in human terms, we do perceive "grades" of greatness, don't we? We just can't help it. People are judging machines, always assessing better and worse, bigger and smaller, more and less. Yet when it comes to The Tap, we're much wiser simply to *listen then act* rather than try to judge how significant something is before we act. The two lines in the Bible right before the one I've paraphrased several times already—from those to whom much is entrusted, much will be expected—offer important instruction. As part of a story he's telling, Jesus reveals:

THAT SERVANT WHO KNOWS his master's will and does not get ready or does not do what his master wants will be beaten with many blows. But the one who does not know and does things deserving punishment will be beaten with few blows.

Kind of harsh, right? But it makes a crucial point: You may once have been in the category of "the one who does not know," but if we're going to apply this parable to The Tap, you must recognize now that you're "the servant who knows." You're now aware of The Tap, and when your next Tap Moment comes, you will be acutely aware of "the master's will." The bad news is that if in the past you were feeling, like so many people I've met, as if life lacked luster, as if something were missing, as if there was some kind of emptiness inside—you were being "beaten with few blows"—now if you choose to *ignore* The Tap, life may very well get even harder for you. Awareness brings greater responsibility. If you aren't ready for this responsibility, then you might do well to close your book right now and instead go read the latest edition of the *National Enquirer* at your favorite checkout counter. . . .

(Still with me? Great, let's go on to the next important piece about what happens to those who know and don't follow through when God calls them.)

Be careful of literalizing here: I don't think God's going to strike you down with a lightning bolt, and this isn't a hellfire-and-brimstone, pound-on-the-pulpit concept. To my mind, it has more to do with the depression, desperation, dissatisfaction, and lack of fulfillment experienced by many people who feel as if there ought to be something more to life—yet they can't quite put their finger on what to do about it.

One study showed that happiness levels are U-shaped over the course of a person's life, with most people bottoming out around middle age. That's probably not a newsflash for you—the midlife crisis is hardly a breakthrough discovery. But I thought it was interesting that they pinpointed it: Universally, based on a sample of more than two million people in eighty countries, depression is at its worst around forty-four years old. (Which happens to be close to my current age. Hmmm.) The good news is that our early years are full of ignorant bliss—yes, youth is king—and we can look forward to bouncing back after we've hit bottom. By the time we're moving back up the curve in our fifties and sixties, if we're still in good shape physically, we can feel as good as we did in our twenties and thirties as we more fully enjoy the rest of our lives.

When asked what they attribute this curve to, one of the authors of the study, an economics professor from the University of Warwick named Andrew Oswald, said its cause is unknown. However, he offered these theories:

ONE POSSIBILITY IS THAT individuals learn to adapt to their strengths and weaknesses, and in mid-life quell their infeasible aspirations. Another possibility is that cheerful people live systematically longer. A third possibility is that a kind of comparison process is at work in which people have seen similar-aged peers die and value more their own remaining years. **Perhaps people somehow learn to count their blessings.** [*Emphasis added.*]

———

Regardless of your age, small taps matter because they point to your blessings, helping you acknowledge what you already have—enough arm strength to carry someone's groceries, some cash in your wallet, a coat on your back, a car to drive, and so on. Responding to The Tap is just one way of "counting" your blessings, acknowledging them and then acting out of your awareness. Doing this over and over again, with both "easy" taps and those you perceive to be more challenging, helps you develop that risk-tolerance muscle and its twin, tap sensitivity. Responding to every tap, no matter what level of significance you may give it, prepares you to recognize more opportunities. That's important, because The Tap doesn't always call you to do exactly what you'd expect.

God doesn't work like an ATM machine. Prayer isn't a push-button. You don't get on your knees one day, asking for greater territory or more blessings of any kind, and—*poof!*—your prayers are answered with some clear request to share of yourself, which obviously correlates to your request, and then you do that thing, and—*poof!*—what you originally wanted materializes, just as if you'd ordered it from a catalog. No, no, no. Prayer is a lot more mysterious than pressing a button or filling out an order form.

It can be tempting to dismiss The Tap when it's really not what you want to hear right now. You can tune it out. "Frank, you wanted to be known as the 'king of ready-made dream homes,' or the 'real estate rock czar' who creates and then sells homes for hundreds of millions, or as a bestselling author many times over. Well, you're going to have to serve meals from the back of a beat-up old van to people who are homeless."

Was that what I wanted to hear? No, I wanted to hear that an amazing deal would manifest itself as quickly as I prayed it would! But that's just not how it works most of the time. Although there's no question that The Tap can call you to do what we'd consider great things—those actions that positively affect many, many lives—sometimes the most personally significant taps come in the form of something you resist, or think is silly, or deem trivial.

In retrospect, I can see how incredibly important responding to the tap that led me to The Caring Kitchen has become. At the time, it seemed like an important change for me to make, but I had no illusions that, by serving meals to people, I was doing some Nobel-prize level good deed. Yet it's easy now for me to look back and say to myself, *Look at the times I have followed through on The Tap—look at what amazing things have happened! Look at how my life has evolved and changed for the better. Look at the enlightenment I have gained.*

If you want to lead a tapped life, embracing all the rewards and responsibilities that includes, then you need to prepare yourself to act on your Tap Moments, large and small, easy and inconvenient. The next time you feel that nudge, remember what one wise Englishman said: "Never regret anything you have done with a sincere affection; nothing is lost that is born of the heart." Today, why not do more than just "be open" to The Tap? Why not be committed to acting on your next Tap Moment the instant you feel it? The very next time you see an opportunity to share what you have with someone, and it's within your means to do so, why not *decide now* to say yes?

Your Chapter 6 *Tap* Moments

- There's no such thing as an insignificant Tap Moment.

- Strive to make "yes" your natural response.

- See every Tap Moment as an opportunity to count your blessings.

- Sometimes, the most personally significant taps come in the form of something you resist, or think is silly, or deem trivial.

- Remember to turn the nine "small" Tap Moment opportunities into a short list to go in your purse or wallet, and see how long it takes you to check them all off as done. Share your results with me and others at The-Tap.com in the blog called "Share Your Tap Moments." Here they are for you again: 1) Replace store merchandise that's been dropped on the floor, 2) graciously accept some kindness from a stranger, 3) carry someone else's purchase out to the car for them, 4) refer a client to a competitor, 5) tip the custodian in the airport and express your thanks, 6) write a thank-you note with gratuity for hotel housekeeping, 7) compliment the cook at a fast-food restaurant and tip $5, 8) let someone with children cut ahead of you in line at the grocery store, and 9) drop some change in someone else's parking meter.

Seven

WHY NOT DRIVE A PURPLE YUGO?

MY WIFE, NILSA, TEASES me for being a "nerd in sheep's cloth-ing," and it's true: I'm a lot less exciting, at least by rock-star standards, than I look. I don't drink, smoke, do drugs, gamble, overeat, oversleep, or womanize. I'm usually in bed by nine and rise at 4:30 AM to work out almost every day. On Sunday I sleep in until 6 AM. It's the one day a week I put on a white shirt, dark pants, and conservative tie, and then we go to church, where I'm an usher with my daughter, Laura, at the 6:45 mass every week. Although I will always be a recovering adrenaline junkie, I don't drive a high-performance car or race motorcycles much anymore. I have two Yugos (an automobile that many who are unaware of its finer qualities refer to as one of the worst/cheapest/slowest cars ever built—a point of view I adamantly refute) and a 2002 hybrid Honda Insight. I walk Laura to school every morning at 7:15 when I'm in town, take my lunch to work in an old lunch box, have the same card-board trash can I've used for thirteen years, don't eat out much, and (as you may have gathered already) go to 7-Eleven a lot. I enjoy an occasional Slurpee.

Like she said: *nerd.*

When I cruise around Delray Beach in my "special-occasion" purple Yugo on date night or on my way to church, I know some people are thinking I'm a bit eccentric. Or in dire straits: "Has the real-estate market gotten so tough, Frank?" They speculate that it must be pretty desperate (and some of them say it, too) if I'm willing to drive a car that supposedly has market value only when you fill the gas tank, and will go fast only when you push it off a cliff.

"And did you see the color? Does he know it's *purple,* for goodness' sake?"

To be precise, it's metallic *plum.* Originally, I bought the car for $600, spent a considerable sum to get it running like new, and then got the can't-miss custom paint job. It still spends a fair share of the time in the shop, but no matter. This finely hued motor vehicle is accessorized with white-wall tires and white faux-alligator interior with purple cloth accents, and I love it! Every other automobile that rolls by my house is a stately, subdued Bentley, Ferrari, Mercedes, or Jaguar. Nobody else has anything like my Yugos. And they're so . . . me, just not the me most people expect.

Throughout my entire life, I've taken a contrarian approach. It's made me money, and it's made my brand as I've created new markets, mostly because I've embraced my individuality and turned that into a calling

My Purple Yugo

Want to enjoy the car in all its glory? Visit The-Tap.com to see a full-color photo.

card instead of keeping it in my back pocket. Those things that used to get me teased or ostracized (my wardrobe with the white leather jacket and matching pants that I wore in high school come to mind) have evolved into trademarks for me. Clothes don't make this man, but I guess they sure do work differently for this man. Like Don King's straight-up 'do or Donald Trump's comb-over, the long hair I've worn most of my adult life has become part of my brand, or "commercial," as Rich DeVos calls it. (He also once told a large gathering at one of my events, "Now that's hair with a purpose.") What's more, when I pull up to posh job sites and charity luncheons in my presidential blue, business-casual Yugo, that makes its own kind of statement. And when you discover that I build both the most expensive houses and the least expensive ones, too, that really starts to show you who I am.

Many charities hold black-tie fundraisers and golf tournaments, but as you can easily guess, this isn't my style. Instead, for the benefit of our Caring House Project Foundation, I strive to create unique experiences for our benefactors. A recent invitation to "Frank McKinney's Ultimate Tour of Extremes: From Rich to Enriched" began like this:

"We feel most alive when experiencing extremes for the first time, in our pursuit to live the dichotomies found in life, not by merely existing in the 'comfort corridor.' "

What did I mean by that? It seems that most of life takes place between those two railroad tracks we travel over time—our "comfort corridor." Also known as the regular, the routine, the rut. Why not step outside? It leads to a fuller life, one with greater perspective. You can invigorate your living through the extremes of life, either seeking them out or simply saying yes to opportunities when they're presented.

The Tour of Extremes gives our donors an immediate and tangible experience of the dichotomies of life while also showing them firsthand who their donations serve. It always includes a tour of our latest masterpiece and often concludes with an overnight stay in Haiti. Think of the contrast! Imagine something like the grand unveiling of Acqua Liana and our characteristically over-the-top festivities, including a heart-stopping show, my three-book launch, top-drawer food, and the custom-concocted "Manalapan Mojito." (My old friend Brian—remember him from the first chapter?—would be amused to see that there wouldn't be any Italian takeout this time!) As usual, it would be the hottest ticket in town, attended by hundreds of people from the media, VIPs, book-industry executives, and million-dollar real estate brokers, each eager to get a look inside the most opulent "green" house ever created.

The final experience, the pièce de résistance, the fulfillment of the promise of participating in the dichotomies of life, would be to board a plane to Port-au-Prince, which is the poorest city in the poorest country of the western hemisphere, to tour the villages our donors have enabled us to build there.

We've taken many trips like this with those who've been both generous in their contribution and delighted to get an insider's look at our mansions. Not long ago, we took such a group to Cité Soleil. On the way, we saw signs of the ravages of poverty everywhere. People living in shacks. Roadside stands selling the mud patties that help stave off hunger. Garbage everywhere, the stench of death and disease. Because desperation also breeds violent crime, few outsiders go to this slum area without being escorted by armored carriers from the United Nations. But we were expected; nearly two hundred former residents of Cité Soleil now live in a village we built on the other side of Port-au-Prince, and the people were so gracious in receiving us. Upon our arrival, one man told us, "Our home is your home." We had a communal meal together before sitting down in front of a warm fire to hear a moving reflection and share conversation with the people from the village. Our donors got to witness firsthand the impact they were having on this desperately poor, but hopeful and happy population.

I venture to say that this part of "Frank McKinney's Ultimate Tour of Extremes: From Rich to Enriched" forever changed the way our guests perceived life. It represented an epiphanous Tap Moment for all.

It's interesting. Almost all the correspondence I've received from those who've attended any of our Tours of Extremes focuses on this last leg of the trip. They rarely mention Acqua Liana, or other oceanfront mansions they are fortunate to see, the grand unveiling parties, or much else. No, they write about how moved they were by the people they met in Haiti. After a recent Tour of Extremes, I heard back from so many people about how they were brought to tears when a small brass band struck up "The Star-Spangled Banner" for the Americans in Cité Soleil. Past participants regularly write to me about the beautiful children, and how much they

God's Beautiful Children

Children at one of the feeding centers in Cité Soleil (the slums of Haiti's capital) display signs that bestow blessings on me as their bon papa, *or "benevolent godfather." It has been my greatest honor to get to know and serve the people here.*

want to continue to support both the newly thriving communities and the ones that are still struggling desperately. They want to know what's next and how they can share God's blessings with those who need it most.

Why do they mention these things and not the "impressive" parts of this Tour of Extremes? Because they now have a better understanding of life's priorities. They're more comfortable with their own mission. They've experienced a powerful Tap Moment. They've come to understand how vital it is to live the paradoxes in life, to get out of that comfort corridor and experience the extremes.

Go on, Take a Joy Ride

I HAVE A pretty good handle on human contrasts, and I like to say I've earned a Ph.D. in "paradoxicology." Demonstrating contrariness within my own personality has also become part of the Frank McKinney brand: the dichotomies of daredevil/Yugo lover, rocker/nerd, rule-breaker/ happily married for twenty years, and $1,200-per-square-foot oceanfront mansions/$12-per-square-foot homes in Haiti are all equally vital parts of me.

This kind of contradiction isn't restricted to me. *Each of us* is made up of intriguing opposites: the quiet accountant who loves professional wrestling, the plainspoken farmer with season tickets to his local Shakespeare theater, the hard-bitten reporter with a secret stash of Hello Kitty collectibles, the angel-voiced customer relations rep who bangs her head to heavy metal on the weekends, the intellectual who loves *MAD* magazine, the high-powered corporate executive whose favorite pastime is scrapbooking.

It all reminds me of an old *Saturday Night Live* commercial parody for a product they called Shimmer. Chevy Chase as the spokesman says, "New Shimmer is both a floor wax and a dessert topping! Here, I'll spray some on your mop [he turns to Gilda Radner and squirts it on] … and some on your butterscotch pudding [he dispenses some on Dan Aykroyd's dessert]."

Dan eats while Gilda mops, and then Dan pipes up, "Mmmmmmm, tastes terrific!"

Gilda: "Just look at that shine! But will it last?"

Chevy/spokesman: "Hey, outlasts every other leading floor wax, two to one. It's durable and it's scuff-resistant."

Dan: "And it's delicious!"

The bit goes on like that, contrasting Shimmer's nonyellowing formula with its ability to perk up anything from an ice cream sundae to a pumpkin pie. It ends with the tagline, "New Shimmer: For the greatest shine you ever tasted!"

This is such a funny and memorable skit because of the unlikely pairing. So let me ask you: What's *your* Shimmer? **What's *your* purple Yugo?** What about you would surprise someone who didn't know you very well? What might strike someone else as out-of-character—but is actually an essential part of who you are? Even more important: *Do you allow yourself to embrace that astonishing thing, that spark of the unexpected?* Or do you keep that shining plum parked in a garage somewhere, hidden and rusting away?

It's all too common for me to meet people who think they have to conceal this part of themselves, whatever it may be. Most of us start pushing down some of our uniqueness when we're kids and try to fit in, and it's easy to get into the habit and never stop doing that. Playground pressure becomes peer pressure becomes societal pressure. It can feel inescapable, inevitable, indelible.

Although I'm definitely not a conformist, this pressure still affects me. Every now and then, I still have that nagging sense that I should just be what someone else wants me to be. When I was working on Acqua Liana and Crystalina, two of our real estate projects focused on environmentally conscious, luxury building, I was being pursued by a well-known cable TV network to star in a docu-series titled *The Green Giant*. After a prolonged courtship, and even the production of a trailer, I was told I wouldn't be a good front man because I'm not "the face of green." How disappointing! I really believed in what we were doing, and I was in the vital process of evolving the Frank McKinney brand to include green building, so for a moment I was tempted to grab a pair of Birkenstocks, chop off some of my hair, and put on a tree hugger T-shirt. But I came to my senses after some reflection about the other times I've tried to wear a uniform and march in lockstep.

There was the time when I was in my early twenties and went to an office seeking my first position in real estate. I'd gone to the barber, put on a new suit and tie, and worn the most uncomfortable shoes I think I've ever had on my feet. After my potential employer called me by the wrong name and told me I needed a different suit, haircut, and pair of shoes that would be more "dignified," I realized that conventional real estate wasn't for me. I walked out of there, kicked off my shoes, and gave my tie to the clerk at the 7-Eleven.

I'd made the same mistake of playing dress up after my father died in a plane crash on September 11, 1992. (Not "the" September 11; it was a few years before that.) Without getting too deeply psychological, I think it's safe to say that I was working out my grief and compensating for my loss when I once again cut my hair and donned a suit, and tried to buy a failed savings and loan on the west coast of Florida. A reporter snapped my picture on the forty-eighth floor of my dad's old office building as I looked out the window at my dad's old bank. I was the spitting image of him that day, and I continued the charade until I finally woke up and asked myself what on earth I was trying to prove. *This will never work, Frank. You have the business sense to pull this off, but this isn't YOU.* Wisely, I dropped it and went back to high-end real estate with its greater risk, higher margins, and my own dress code.

All this to say: I've been there. I've felt the riptide and resisted it. That's mainly because I know nothing crushes your spirit more nor keeps you confined to a smaller version of yourself than hiding your true self away. Likewise, nothing makes you more interesting and attractive (in a universal sense) than exposing all of you, including your eccentricities: both the parts that your friends, family, and society at large probably condone and the parts that they might think are wacky, irresponsible, immature, uncool, or otherwise unconventional.

Suppression of intriguing quirks and idiosyncrasies is like personality undertow. Unless you allow them to surface, the real you can get sucked under and drown in a sea of conformity. If you're looking to find your passion and place in the world, don't co-opt or change your essential self for anyone or anything. If you want to be joyful and ready for your next Tap Moment, then rejoice in what makes you different and accentuate it.

What might happen if you allowed whatever's been dragged under to come up for some air? I bet that, in addition to having more fun, you'd breathe new life into your ability to feel The Tap. If you've suffocated your ability to recognize and honor *your own* needs, you can't expect to be sensitive to those of other people. There's a marked difference in emotional maturity between someone who allows the prevailing culture to restrict him or her because of what "they" think, and someone who defines himself or herself and thereby has the power to influence the people and culture at large.

If you find yourself thinking, *No, there's no purple Yugo for me,* then I invite you to pay more attention to what brings you that little shiver of excitement, probably something you've intentionally ignored in the past. If there's something "off" that delights you, and maybe it amuses you to recognize how much you really, really like it—that's the thing. That's your purple Yugo.

As long as that thing is good for you and good for others, you'd be wise to cherish it and start letting yourself have it. Have you always loved Vivaldi, Van Halen, or Van Morrison but been embarrassed to admit it for some reason? Wanted to wear cowboy boots or a flak jacket or leather pants but didn't think you could pull it off? Wished you could tell people that you're into hardboiled crime fiction or Harlequin romance novels? Kept your test-tube collection or mad nunchuck skills hush-hush? Harbored a secret desire to learn how to use a pogo stick or shoot a bow and arrow? Would you love to raise a flock of turkeys or speak a dying language or dance flamenco-style?

Is there something you'd truly enjoy that would cause someone to say, "Really? *You?* You're into *that?!*" These are the kinds of "temptations" you want to give in to; they're actually good for the soul and enliven your whole being.

The Seven Deadly Distractions

JUST AS IMPORTANT as it is for you to "drive your purple Yugo," whatever your purple Yugo may be, it's also crucial to be aware of the indulgences that aren't in your best interests. You may already know what these are for you. Figuring that out for myself is what a large part of my misspent youth was about. It's also why, as flamboyant as my outward appearance may be now, I've become quite circumspect in and protective of my private life. I've done my best to give up all those things that have the potential to deaden me to The Tap.

Do you need some help figuring out what might be problematic for you? One useful guide comes from the Roman Catholic Church, which classifies the most destructive vices, which we'll call the "seven deadly distractions," into three types, those of the:

- **Appetite**, including 1) lust/sexual compulsion, 2) gluttony/overconsumption, and 3) greed

- **Temperament**, including 4) sloth/indifference and 5) wrath/rage
- **Intellect**, including 6) envy and 7) pride

Even for those who aren't Catholic or Christian, it's useful to take a look at this list from time to time and see which ones you can consider "done" (as in not hanging over you, over with, finished, kaput, not an issue) and which ones still create internal struggles for you. As I mentioned, I don't indulge any of the habits that are commonly known to be addictive, other than my need for an occasional adrenaline "drip" that has replaced the rush—those are off-limits to me because I know they could completely sidetrack me, so they're checked off the list. Yet I'm hardly "done" with the whole list. *Greed, temperament, and temptation—* that's my personal shorthand helping me remember where the traps are for me and which parts of my personality have the potential for getting me into trouble and desensitizing me to The Tap.

All You, All the Time?

ALTHOUGH I'VE MADE much of my public and private life transparent by writing this and other books, I'm not necessarily recommending that you do it. You certainly don't have to share everything about yourself with everyone you meet; I don't. Because you're reading this right now (and if you've read the others I've written), you know more about me than most people who *think* they know me based on media coverage. I'm always a little puzzled by the ones who express suspicion about how my private life is much different from my public image, especially that it's a lot less flash and much more substance. I have to ask these folks, "Do you really expect me to look the same at a grand unveiling as I do sitting on my couch at home? Am I supposed to wear a bright red jacket and leopard-print pants when I watch *SpongeBob SquarePants* with my daughter?" I don't get that. Why would that make me somehow more authentic? Isn't it more real to admit there are several sides to me, and to let all of them have their place and time?

More to the point, it's okay with me if my public image has a life of its own that isn't completely reflective of the private me. In the public eye, I've chosen to emphasize the part of my personality that tends to prefer the theatrical. If I could sing, then maybe I'd be the singing real estate guy, but I can't, so I'm not. Instead, I work with what I've got to attract the one buyer I need from the only 50,000 people who can afford the artistry I create. I've chosen to accentuate my theatrical side to draw attention to what is really being sold. Which isn't me, nor is it the goofy theatrics. It's the masterpiece behind the front door.

Similarly, I've met Tony Little, the hyped-up exercise enthusiast who sells equipment like a barker at a carnival—and what do you know? He's quiet and shy. When he shakes your hand, he doesn't yell or point at your "BUT-tocks." Thank goodness. He's a normal guy with a very distinctive brand. I can assure you, that's the case with most people in the public eye.

Here's just one more example from the hundreds I could give you: In person, Don King, who I mentioned earlier, is hardly the screaming, hyperbolic, power promoter that you see in the ring before a fight.

When he was looking at one of our properties for sale, Nilsa and I took Don and his wife, Henrietta, out to dinner. We went into the restaurant through the back door and ate in a private room with a body guard standing in the corner (for him, not me). It was just the five of us there, so I came out and asked him, "Don, what's up with the hair?"

He gave me a look that said, *Hello! I could ask you the same question.* But he told me, "Well, Frank, it's a distinguishing physical characteristic."

I let it drop after that, but I suspect that he meant that if it weren't for him waving our country's flag and wearing his sequined jean jackets and smiling that big smile of his with his hair sticking straight up, he'd be just another fight promoter. The man *works* that style: On his headquarters building in Deerfield Beach, Florida, he has the biggest American flag you'll ever see and his logo is the word *Don* with spikes flaring off the top of it, reminiscent of both a crown and Don's signature 'do.

Beyond the bluster of his brand, though, I found Don to be incredibly kind and gentle, particularly with his wife. Over dinner, he talked with us about how much he loved her, and he was obviously deeply devoted. He and Henrietta were lovely company that night—and nothing at all like his public image, a controversial sports figure who likes to mix it up and dish it out.

It's okay for you, too, to develop a "brand" or "commercial" that's not the whole story but instead an amplified version of just one part of you. In fact, I think it's beneficial to the healthy development of ego and self-confidence. Yet you are more than your brand. The whole point of this chapter is to encourage you to bring out all parts of yourself in the time and place that make the most sense for you. It's to encourage you to try new things (or old things you've neglected) that will be enjoyable and delightful and unexpected. The purple Yugo is a metaphor, obviously, for whatever you believe to be the antidote to the person the rest of the world thinks they see. Hollywood and even reality TV are always looking for the "central character who plays against type," and your purple Yugo makes you a shining star, demonstrating that you are far more than the one or two things other people expect you to be.

You may have picked up this book because you recognized Tap Moments as a path to spiritual enlightenment. What I'm hoping to convey is that driving a purple Yugo is a critical part of that same path. Giving yourself permission to embrace the fullness of who you are—unpopular, unexpected, and unconventional included—is part and parcel of The Tap. Whether you choose to bring out these parts of you every day and in a public way, or to enjoy them sporadically and privately, makes no difference; they're an important part of joyful giving. Being unique, having fun, being unpredictable—celebrating everything that makes you "shimmer"—can be just as important as doing the serious work of service to others.

Back in 1903, when the first Crayola kids' crayons hit the market, the box included eight colors: black, brown, blue, red, purple, orange, yellow, and green. In 1958, they upped it to "64 Brilliant Colors" and introduced that little sharpener on the back of the box. Today, there are hundreds of different crayons, including those that glow in the dark, have sparkles, change colors, smell like flowers, and sharpen themselves. My point is that all of those crayons are special. I have a favorite—magenta—and you probably have one, too (the most popular color is blue), but when you open a new box, not often does one color really stand out. I like to think of people as being like kids' crayons: In the box, we don't seem so special. Out of the box, look out! It's your choice if you remain unopened and unused. My advice is that you get out of the box, sharpen your ability to feel The Tap, and allow God to color something majestic and wonderful and compellingly original with you.

YOUR CHAPTER 7 *Tap* MOMENTS

• Consider how other people see you . . . What in your personality or behavior contradicts that public image? What is your purple Yugo?

• Think about how you might magnify and celebrate what makes you different. Embrace that astonishing thing, that spark of the unexpected.

• Start satisfying your own unmet needs and see how quickly this increases your awareness of what other people need.

• Identify your top three of life's "seven deadly distractions." Can you pinpoint those that have the potential to deaden your sensitivity to The Tap? Merely creating an awareness of them now will help you resist the temptation in the future.

• Develop a personal brand, but also realize that you are more than the public image. Be sure to take that purple Yugo out for a spin!

• Take a moment to have some fun with Crayola.com. Go online and choose your favorite color. You'll be amused by what that says about you!

Eight

PACK THIS IN YOUR LUNCH PAIL

EVERY MORNING WHEN I arrive at one of our oceanfront job sites and pull the keys out of the ignition, put my leg out of the car, and then grab my old, tattered lunch box, I have this moment of what I can only call *solace*. It's not the magnificence of the project or the property or the view that brings me that feeling, though. It's the lunch box . . . such a simple thing, a mundane and practical thing, but somehow it's beautiful to me.

I'm not exaggerating: My business philosophy can even be summed up in that one item. It symbolizes to me the day-in, day-out efforts that move you toward your ultimate professional or spiritual highest calling. It's the sheer act of showing up, executing what needs to be done, staying focused on the big picture at all times. When people talk about overnight successes, as they frequently did earlier in my career, I always think of the truth, tucked away like so many sandwiches and carrots over thousands of days, that led up to that point in time: **The big reward may seem to have appeared all of a sudden, but it's really the result of doing the job, doing it well, and doing it every single day.** Perhaps it was through my lack of formal education that I came to rely on the simplicity found in just showing up each day to do my best. It was all I could fall back on in my early days. It served me well, so I decided never to abandon the approach.

Plenty of people recommend that you make long-range plans for success, and then break it down into shorter milestones. I come from the school of having a long-range vision of success—and making it something that sounds slightly impossible even to you—but then making plans only for the shorter term. In my view, close, achievable milestones are best for individuals. Leave the three-, five-, and ten-year plans to the Fortune 500. (Heck, if you've read *Good to Great* by Jim Collins, which I strongly endorse, you know that spending more time on long-range strategic planning doesn't make all that much difference even in the big companies.) As an entrepreneur and a maverick who likes to keep my options open and my game fluid, I don't create plans for anything farther out than a year. Sure, I have some big *goals*— ideas about the kind of person I'd like to become and the great things I'd like to be, do, have, and give—but I keep my eyes focused on the part of the road I can see from here. Success coach and author Jack Canfield has made the analogy of the headlights on a car that show you only two hundred feet ahead. Everything beyond that is dark, and if you try to drive by looking into the pitch black, you'll crash, plain and simple. But if you keep your eyes on that piece of road that's lit up right in front of you, you can travel quite a distance.

The ultramarathon I've run several times, the Badwater, sounds like an incredible feat to many people—something out there in that blackness beyond the headlights. Often, I hear, "There's no way I could do that, Frank." But they could. I know they could. (The average age of the participants is forty-seven, and the oldest is seventy!) Maybe 135 miles sounds impossible, but could you walk or run *one* mile—and then do it 135 times? Of course! But if you've never done it before, conceiving of the whole thing at once makes your knees knock, at least if you have any sense. Similarly, once you're in that race, it's a death sentence to start thinking about the end when you're only at mile 26 (equivalent to a regular marathon) and still have 109 miles in 130-degree heat to the finish. The thing that will keep you going is to focus on *taking the next step,* and on achieving very short milestones, like getting to the next mile marker, or to that cactus just up ahead. You simply have to keep moving forward. In fact, I have inscribed in chalk over the window in the sauna, directly in front of my treadmill: RELENTLESS FORWARD MOTION. It's one of those truisms that applies not just to physical endurance and excellence, but to business, and to the business of life.

In the Badwater Ultramarathon itself, the goal is no wasted effort; again, it's relentless forward motion. Most of us on the road don't even stop for bathroom breaks—we've figured out how to take care of business while we're on the move. It's tough but it's worth it; the time you'd lose otherwise would add up. We're drinking a tremendous amount of water to stay hydrated (more than thirteen gallons in a forty-eight-hour period), and too-frequent pit stops could easily tack on hours to your final time and even cost you the finishers' prize of a Badwater belt buckle. So even when it's incredibly inconvenient, awkward, and unattractive, you keep going.

Here's another reason I know most people could do the race: To finish Badwater—and the goal for most of us is finishing, not winning—in the required sixty hours, you can average around 2.25 miles an hour, which is about the pace of a casual walk. To earn the coveted belt buckle, you need to maintain 2.81 miles an hour. Yet many people don't finish at all, and I'll tell you why. They start out too fast. They don't pace themselves. They zigzag, crossing the road and wasting steps; they stop to eat and chat and piddle around; the relentless-forward-motion mantra isn't there. At some point, the body gets hyperfatigued and sleep-deprived, and since the mental game was lost miles ago, they're out. Since the inception of this epic race in 1977, only about 65 percent of the ninety entrants selected to participate in each race actually finish.

That's a lot like life, isn't it? People get excited about something, go great guns, and then they drop out long before the finish line. But those who do make it, especially those who make it big, start relatively small and build over time, pacing themselves and making incremental progress. Whether we're talking about running a race, parenting a child, building a business, or just mowing the lawn, steady progress is the name of the game. "Slow and steady" isn't the sexiest idea you've ever heard, but it's definitely the most surefire route to success in any endeavor. Even the book you hold in your hands reflects the slow composition of nearly 75,000 words brought together with careful thought over the course of a year. Undertaking writing any worthwhile book may seem like a daunting task, but I bet you could write two hundred words a day, and after a year you'd have your own story to tell.

Once, when I was talking with friend and writer Karen Risch about the challenges of her profession, and my own challenge of completing three books simultaneously, she gave me this great piece of advice about how never to suffer from writer's block again: Keep going. Even. If. It's. One. Word. A. Minute. The second you give in to "I can't," "I don't know," "I won't figure it out,"—all the same stuff that comes into your head whenever you're challenged in any situation—the minute you give in to that, it's over. You have to pack up for the day. So just keep at it; squeeze out what you can squeeze out, and then soon you'll gain momentum again.

Keep plugging along. Keep showing up. Grab your lunch pail and get ready for another day. Feeling The Tap and succeeding in the business of life is all about small steps: *relentless forward motion.*

Stop Dreaming and Start Doing

THIS BOOK ISN'T about dreams and dreamers but about real people pursuing a meaningful vision for their lives. Most dreams are something we have when we're asleep anyway, and they rarely come true in real life. Instead, *The Tap* calls you to action, not reverie. Great aspirations will manifest, but you've got to start small and build. By acting on your Tap Moments, an enlarged reality is attainable one small scene at a time. Already in this book, I've asked you to choose some simple, easily accessible acts of kindness to do. That was to get you in the mood and the mindset of taking the first step. Now I hope to help you establish a habit of sharing yourself day in and day out, not necessarily coming up with a plan to save the world, but instead making the necessary moves toward helping others in whatever way you can.

So let me say it another way: Don't take on too big of a challenge. Choose one that's the right size for where you are today. When someone with interest but no practical experience in real estate wants my advice, my counsel is always the same: **Start with *one* deal that's on a scale that pushes you, but not so much you can't manage it. When you've successfully completed that one and learned from it, do the next one. And then the next.** And so on. There's no get-rich-quick element to my strategies for success. They're actually kind of boring when you boil them down: As I said earlier, do the job, do it well, and do it every day.

If you were to attempt the big deal first, you'd probably crash and burn. It's like the lottery winners who become instant millionaires only to become nearly-as-instant bankruptcy filers. They lose their money for all kinds of reasons—gambling, lawsuits, bad investments, spending sprees, even giving it away indiscriminately—but the common thread, I think, is a lack of preparation for the ascent, a missing mindset and a deficiency of experience with handling the smaller amounts first. There was no lunch pail approach, just sudden wealth.

When I began my career in real estate, I started out with the $50,000 fixer-upper and worked my way up. I didn't magically acquire the ability to manage these multimillion-dollar projects, the deals didn't just fall in my lap, and although there may have been some luck involved, I had as much bad as good. I worked hard, learned the business, did my property research, educated myself about the local markets, and then made my own markets. That was a process of nearly twenty-five years, not the result of me hitting a jackpot or using some trick to get big dollars with little effort or skill.

I don't mind sounding like somebody's grandpa when I say it: **Diligent work pays off.** If you decide to embrace your Tap Moments whenever they come, every time they come, you'll experience the greatest reward possible. If you choose to dabble in The Tap, to respond to the call every now and then or whenever you feel like it, then expect the rewards to be as sporadic as your efforts.

As you've read before, each time you say to yourself, *Yes, God, sign me up,* you increase your tap sensitivity and, if you do it regularly, you're likely to be called to greater and more challenging types of service. Soon, you become a conduit of Tap Moments for other people, either inspiring them to do something for someone else, or being the recipient of their kindness. For example, when you decide to participate in a charity walkathon or race, and you tap the people around you for contributions, what do you think is really going on? It's as if you take God's hand, and together you touch your friends and family on the shoulder, saying, "Hey, what about you? Wouldn't you like to share something, too?"

No matter how large your circle of influence becomes, and how significant you start to think your contributions are, it's always crucial to continue to take the so-called small actions, to express thanks to someone who doesn't usually hear it, to help out a friend who needs it, to volunteer for community service of some kind, to pony up some cash for a good cause. Not only are these just as important in God's eyes as wider-reaching actions, but they also ground you, keeping your head out of the clouds and right here on earth with the people you love the most.

A Thousand Walks to School

MY DAUGHTER, LAURA, and I walk to school together every morning of the school year. We take a one-mile path from our house through a dense grove of trees, past a nature preserve, and over a drawbridge on the Intracoastal Waterway. We pick up a rock or shell every day to commemorate our walk, so you can imagine we have quite a collection. The only time I'm forced to skip this ritual is when I'm out of town, and then Laura walks with Nilsa. Since prekindergarten, Laura has never been driven to school. Most of the time, just a couple of Laura's friends come with us. They all have special nicknames: Laura is Ppeekk (pronounced "Peekie") and her friends are "Mini Romey" and "Quatro." On the first Friday of every month, we have a bigger crowd—our record has been forty kids on the walk to school—because everyone in Laura's class, and even kids from other grades, are invited to come, as long as they get to our house by seven in the morning.

What's the big deal? Why would so many want to walk to school with us once a month, and why am I so committed to walking with Laura every single day that I can?

For the kids, the answer's simple: *It's fun.* I discipline them only if someone's in real danger. We do things they'd never do otherwise, like our "Roadkill Ritual," where everyone lays down in the middle of the road, defying the usual admonitions to "get out of the street!" We invent stories about what we see on the way, like the time we came across a very flat, very dead shiner fish, who we dubbed King Frederick IX. We made up a nickname and his backstory: "Dead Fred" is the deposed king of High Voltage, an underwater world populated by talking manatees, hip-hop dolphins, opera-singing starfish, and practical-joking clownfish who encourage children to launch their school lunch boxes off the bridge. (This part of the story was the result of me allowing the kids to pitch their lunch boxes off the bridge, seeing who could get closest to a T-shaped rock. The closer your lunch box lands, the more points you earn, and at the end of the year, the winner gets a twenty-second shopping spree at—where else?—7-Eleven. Most of the kids could care less about the prize, though, and just love throwing their lunch boxes off the bridge.) Dead Fred has a nemesis, of course, this Megalodon, a monster prehistoric shark with blood-sucking remoras hanging off of him. They've taken over High Voltage and are sucking the joy out of any human who crosses their path! So, on any given day, we could be on a mission to save Dead Fred and avoid the Megalodon and his henchmen, or maybe we're imagining another caper. Our main goal is to have a good time on the way to school, so it's no wonder the kids absolutely love it.

As for me, the reason is a little more complex. It's about spending time with my daughter, being there for her consistently and completely,

Walking to School

"The Roadkill Ritual": Forty kids doing something that would freak out most parents.

making sure there's a part of the day she can count on seeing her dad, playing with him, and having adventures together. It's also my chance to have fun and get to know my daughter's friends. I see their world; I enter their world; I feel what it's like to be a kid again. I will never lose the little boy inside, and I hope you never lose your own sense of child-like joy and wonder and whimsy either.

On another level, I'm also making a point, one that's reflected in the young readers' fantasy and adventure novel I'm writing, which I mentioned earlier. *Dead Fred, Flying Lunchboxes, and the Good Luck Circle* will be released at the exact same time as *The Tap* and the other book I'm working on (one on real estate investment strategies called *Burst This! Frank McKinney's Bubble-Proof Real Estate Strategies*). For the kids who read *Dead Fred,* they get to experience our adventures vicariously and in their full glory, as I've really let loose in creating the fictional characters and their escapades. For the adults, there's a potent message about our grown-up society, which tends to be self-consumed. The story encourages us, as parents, not to lose the little girl or boy inside and to allow our children to just be kids, to feed their imaginations and sense of joy. It's the parenting corollary to the "lunch pail approach": keeping in touch with the child's world through constant contact, shaping and guiding and protecting through regular time together, having an impact on the development of character and worldview by sharing values through imaginative play.

In other words, I've been tapped to write the story of Dead Fred. I walk with Laura because I'm her dad and I love being with her. We include the rest of the kids who come with us on the walk because it's an opportunity for Laura and me to share our blessings of time, fun, and creativity. These children crave what we do and have and are together.

Our real-life adventures are potent reminders of how easy it is to make a difference in a child's life. I'll never forget the Friday that one of the girls pitched her lunch off the bridge and the Velcro sack burst open, scattering dozens of goldfish crackers in the water. Although Candace often wore a sad face (her parents were in the middle of a brutal divorce), she burst out in peals of laughter. Suddenly, a huge pelican came out of nowhere and gulped down all the crackers, along with the rest of her lunch. "Whooooah!" All the kids thought that was so cool! And when we arrived at our usual stop-off (yes, 7-Eleven), and more than twenty-five kids were picking out their treats, Candace arrived at the counter with three goodies, although normally each child can have *one* of whatever he or she wants.

Forgetting what had happened just fifteen minutes earlier, I told her, "Honey, one thing, please."

"But Mr. McKinney, my sandwich is gone and all my goldfish . . ." She started to look worried.

"Oh, right! Go ahead and get that stuff." I smiled. She smiled. All was well.

When we got to school, Candace was beaming after our morning's outing. Not only did she have exactly what she wanted to eat later, she and her former lunch had been the stars of the day; they'd stolen the show. Having seen Candace's extra glow, her teacher came to me and said, "You have no idea what those walks to school do for that little girl. If it weren't for you and the way you let them play and be children, I don't know where she would be."

What a lovely thing for her to say. It was kind and considerate and caring for her to notice that her student was having a hard time and to acknowledge what I was doing to help. That one walk to school was important to Candace. Yet the bigger picture is that, if I hadn't taken more than a thousand walks to school with Laura, if we hadn't made that same crazy journey so many times before and after that single day, it never would have happened. I'm convinced that the cumulative effect of doing your job, doing it well, and doing it every single day is a *miracle*. Do all those days add up to something miraculous? Yes, they do. And every now and then, do you have a golden day, a day that makes a profound difference for someone? Yes, you do. Thank God.

Seriously, thank God. The lunch pail approach is one part *gratitude*—acknowledgment that you have the wherewithal to take step after step and to take every one of them all the way to the finish line—and one part *determination* that you will do what it takes to build a life of purpose and meaning and fulfillment. So, as you turn the page to the next chapter, feel good in knowing that The Tap grows stronger through many small steps. Developing your sensitivity will take some time, but that's okay. Find solace in the fact that you don't need to change overnight, but the cumulative effect of acting on every Tap Moment will leave you glowing in the character that is . . . tapped.

YOUR CHAPTER 8 *Tap* MOMENTS

- What do you do, do well, and do every single day? What kind of payoff do you see for your diligence?

- What's your version of the $50,000 fixer-upper? What is an action you can take, a commitment you can make, that's on a scale that pushes you but that you can manage?

- Likewise, what is your Badwater race? I bet you can finish it if you break it down into small increments.

- For one week, decide that you will be faithful in responding to The Tap. Whenever you're called, take action. That's right: For every Tap Moment, you'll take the opportunity to share in some way. This will require discipline, and there may be times when you're thinking it's a bore or a chore or you just plain don't want to. But do it anyway! Try the lunch pail approach and choose to show up without fail.

Nine

THE MICROWAVE PRAYER

IF YOU'RE LIKE ME, you might find yourself standing in front of a microwave oven sometime every day. You press the timer buttons, hit "start," and then wait for your lunch, or your popcorn, or whatever. What do you do then? Do you stare at the clock as it counts down to the *ding!* when your food's done?

The "Microwave Prayer" (or "Meditations on a Microwave," if you prefer) is a practice I started so I could make better use of those moments during the day when I'm captive to some mindless task. Instead of just standing there, thoughts wandering, eyes fixed on some meaningless clock, I like to take those couple of minutes to offer a completely unstructured, free-form, quickie prayer. (I hear it's better for your health not to stare at the "nuclear reactor," anyway.) My communication with God usually goes something like this:

"Hi, God. Good week so far. I really love how well my new books are being received, and thanks so much for bringing our new oceanfront project ever closer to a beautiful completion and ultimate sale. Thanks for being there for my daughter last night—she really needed you."

I might pause for a few seconds and picture all of the small but meaningful spiritual moments in my mind's eye, letting my appreciation fill me up. When I'm ready, I continue, "Thank you, Lord, for the opportunity to share my blessings with those less fortunate through our Caring House Project Foundation, thank you for my awareness of The Tap, and thank you for those challenges you place before me that further strengthen my faith in you."

Ding! The microwave tells me my lunch is done, I say amen, and then I'm back out trying to spin the globe.

You can do this in front of the microwave, too. You can also do it when you're:

- Waiting in line or on hold
- Watching your computer go through its paces while a program opens
- Riding in an elevator
- Going to the bathroom
- Standing at the cash register waiting to sign a charge slip
- Brushing your teeth or hair
- Showering
- Lathering-rinsing-repeating
- Idling at a stop light
- Letting your Yugo warm up

• Walking to and from your mailbox

• Making coffee

• Any of the other occasions when you have just a few moments to "tap in"

You can say a prayer, or you can close your eyes and "feel" a thank you to God, or sing a sacred song to yourself, or meditate, or say a mantra. Your aim is to create that spiritual connection. It's to carve out a piece of your *attention,* which some of us find more challenging, at least in the beginning, than finding time in the day for these short devotionals.

The point is *not* to expect God to tap you in that moment. That probably won't happen. This is about taking a pause in your everyday activities to reach out to your creator. Just as in human relationships, you strengthen your relationship with God by sharing downtime, just "hanging out." You also heighten your sensitivity to The Tap by sharing your thoughts and feelings with God.

This is so simple that I need to caution you not to dismiss it as too easy or trivial. It's a wonderful practice that integrates your awareness of Tap Moments and the importance of God's hand in your life.

YOUR CHAPTER 9 *Tap* MOMENT

• Choose at least one time during the day when you can perform a simple prayer or meditation. Then do it!

Ten

THINK FAST,
ACT FASTER

WHEN WE WERE ON tour promoting *Frank McKinney's Maverick Approach* (remember the large rock 'n' roll bus with the book cover and a giant image of my face on all four sides?), I kept asking my new buddy Tom Denman to let me take the wheel.

"Come on, Tom, let me drive the thing!"

Every time I'd ask, he'd wave me off, saying, "Oh, you'll get your chance." Then he wouldn't mention anything more about it.

Not that he'd stop talking altogether. Tom had plenty of tales, and I once told him that if anyone ought to write a book, it was him. But you know how it is when you spend every day with someone? Sometimes you need a break. I often "coincidentally" had a conference call in the back of the bus not long after he got started with some story. I'd leave my assistant Mark with Tom to pretend to politely listen to the rest.

Tom wasn't fooled. He loved to tease Mark, insisting we eat at Cracker Barrel if there was one anywhere near a stop we needed to make (Tom loved the place as much as Mark hated it) and regularly skewering Mark with off-color humor. Mark was a good sport about Tom's ribbing. Mostly.

About a month into the tour, when Tom was driving us through a desert in the southwest—I think we were in Arizona—it was pretty quiet on the bus; no one had said a word for about two hours. I was at my desk, working on my computer, and Mark was watching reruns of *The A-Team.* We were cruising along at about seventy-five miles an hour on one of those long, wide-open straightaways.

Without warning, Tom *got up from his seat, turned his back on the road, and strolled toward the lounge.* He pointed at me and said, casually, "Well, you been askin'. Now's yer chance."

I wasn't anywhere near the front, where Mark was sitting, alone, beside the empty driver's seat. When Mark heard Tom's voice break the silence and then noticed he wasn't at the wheel anymore, he screamed— that high-pitched scream girls in cartoons make when they see a mouse. At the same time, I saw him put his right hand under his rectum, just like an animal tucks its tail when it's terrified.

By then, I was *running* to the front of the bus. (I heard later that Tom never even turned around until he got to the back, and then he did a slow 180 and leeeeeaned up against the refrigerator, twenty-five feet from the steering wheel!) I grabbed the wheel and did my best to steady the huge vehicle as I sat down. Mark vacated his usual seat (maybe he ran to the bathroom?), and I was feeling pretty lonely and terrified until

Tom slowly sauntered up and slid into the seat beside me. He didn't say a thing for a few minutes but would reach over and adjust the wheel every now and then to keep the bus from veering too far one way or the other. I was shaking for the first few minutes, because, number one, Tom had never given me any indication he'd ever *really* let me drive, nor had he given me any instruction whatsoever. Number two, even the slightest wind was swaying the bus.

As I was driving, Tom eventually taught me how to anticipate the wind's effects and where to keep the front left tire in relation to the white line in the road. When I finally relaxed and started laughing about what he'd done, I told him that he obviously had nerves of steel if he was willing to put me at the wheel of a $3 million bus with no training (I drive a Yugo, for heaven's sake), no warning, and while the thing was *moving* at 75 mph! His nonchalance was impressive, and this had to have been the best, possibly the most dangerous, practical joke anyone has ever pulled on me.

Tom just smiled, patted the dashboard, and asked, "Pretty sweet, ain't she?"

Stop Overthinking

GOD DOESN'T DEMAND perfection but rewards obedience and action. We're expected to take the wheel, even if we still need a tremendous amount of help, even if we're scared, even if we didn't expect to be driving at all. But when an opportunity presents itself, we're supposed to run, not walk, to get into the driver's seat.

My Book-Tour Bus, a Home Away From Home

This was the luxury tour bus we used for my second book tour as I made 110 appearances and did 212 bookstore drop-by signings. I probably drove ten (hair-raising) miles, and Tom logged about 12,700 behind the wheel. Look for a newer version on the road in support of The Tap.

Understand that I'm not talking about making stupid choices based solely on enthusiasm. I'm talking about having a baseline of knowledge and making the necessary assessments, but not overanalyzing and debating with yourself and making things more complicated than they really are. I did know how to drive, after all, just not a tour bus. Tom knew that. He also knew I loved to get my adrenaline pumping. And in that moment after Tom said it was time, do you think I sat and thought about whether someone else would be better equipped, or if Mark should take over, or if I ought to jump out the window and take my chances that way? No, I did the thing I knew I could do: I sprinted to the front of the bus, took control, and started driving.

In his excellent book, *Blink*, author Malcolm Gladwell uncovered how some of our best actions come from the swiftest analyses. It turns out that additional information can give you an inflated sense of confidence and actually reduce your ability to make a good decision. One case study was the life-or-death scenario of cardiologic diagnoses. As it turns out, doctors make better decisions about how to treat patients that seem to be having a heart attack if they know less about the patient, not more. Yet, he reports, there's a kind of "automatic tendency among physicians to believe that a life-or-death decision has to be a difficult decision."

It's such a perfect example of how belaboring something is a bad idea, plain and simple. Consider that cardiologists spend four years in undergraduate education (where they study some science, including biology and chemistry), four years in medical school (where they study only medical sciences), three years in residency (practicing hands-on with patients, doing internal medicine), and another three years in fellowship (specifically practicing cardiology). If they then were to overthink every heart-attack diagnosis—taking a couple days to mull it over and hear all their friends' and family's opinions, for instance—they could kill someone. And if they weighed in too many factors and came up with the wrong diagnosis, they could kill someone. An undesirable outcome in either case. With a baseline of knowledge, you need only essential information and the willingness to act so that you can save someone's life.

Decisions aren't always a matter of life and death for most of us. Or are they? They're certainly always a matter of *life*. Consider Allie, a woman who had been an executive with a midsized successful software firm that was bought out by one of the giants. When her position was cut, she saw this as an opportunity to redefine herself, to attempt something altogether different, to figure out her calling in life and pursue that. For the first couple of months, it was like vacation—Allie didn't worry herself about it, but she read a lot of books about purpose, passion, and personal development. This got her interested in taking a few courses on the same subjects, and finding her professional calling became her full-time focus. She attended seminars. She listened to audiotapes. She read still more books. She worked a couple of jobs to make a little money, but they weren't even close to the mark for her.

Two years, dozens of self-help seminars, and several thousand dollars later, Allie still had no idea what she wanted to do for a living.

If I were to make a quick diagnosis, I'd say she was suffering from the proverbial paralysis by analysis. She was so intent on doing the right thing, the perfect thing, that she got caught up in the "seeking" and lost sight of the "finding." **Sometimes, you just gotta run to the front and take the wheel, whether or not you know exactly how to drive the bus.** You never know where you'll end up.

Think about the story of Jesus calling his disciples at the Sea of Galilee. The fishermen were out with their nets in the water, and Jesus said to them—*tap!*—"Follow me, and I will make you fishers of men." Simon and Andrew came "at once," and later, when Jesus called James and John from their boat, these two came "immediately," leaving their father. When you read this story, it's easy for a modern person to skip past the words *at once* and *immediately*. But they're vitally important, especially when you understand that none of these men were fly-by-night, act-on-a-whim kind of guys. Fishing had probably been the family profession for generations as far back as they could remember. Making a speedy decision to completely alter the course of their lives was clearly inspired. None of them were angels, either; each had done things no one would be proud of. This passage of the Bible reinforces the rightness of swift action and the reality that *anyone* can be tapped when they least expect it.

Oftentimes, overthinking is just another way of saying no. You can analyze, and scrutinize, and fantasize . . . and *nothing* actually gets done. By default, making no decision has the same consequences as a decision to say no. Sometimes, you can do this consciously, using your criteria and your spreadsheets and your checklists as a stall tactic; it's frequently unconscious, however, so you're wise to ask yourself if that's what's going on whenever you're putting off making a decision. Given the passage of enough time when pondering a yes or no decision, you will often find a way, conscious or not, to say no. You may find it hard to believe, but you were actually seeking the no all along, and after enough research and deliberation, you justified it. Are you getting stuck because you think there's only one right answer? Remind yourself that there are always at least two right answers. Which would you rather do, err on the side of caution, or err on the side of enthusiasm? Would you rather mistake a mundane moment for The Tap, or miss a Tap Moment because you deliberated and dismissed it? Don't overthink; instead, overdo.

Simplicity, Simplicity, Simplicity

IN THE MID-1800s, Henry David Thoreau published *Walden.* The second chapter, called "Where I Lived, and What I Lived For," could have been written yesterday. Consider this passage:

OUR LIFE IS FRITTERED away by detail. An honest man has hardly need to count more than his ten fingers, or in extreme cases he may add his ten toes, and lump the rest. Simplicity, simplicity, simplicity! I say, let your affairs be as two or three, and not a hundred or a thousand; instead of a million count half a dozen, and keep your accounts on your thumb nail ... Simplify, simplify.

I say he could have written it yesterday because today we are so bombarded by details that it's easy to start believing we need them. It's just another symptom of hyper-analysis: We think we need to *know* everything in order to *do* anything. But we don't! People sometimes imagine that when I say this, I'm talking only about our personal lives, but I'm not. It's another one of my boring business principles: Cut to the chase as quickly as possible, take action, and don't look back. I'm a longtime student and admirer of those who make intelligent, rapid-fire decisions. These people are able to quickly parse a situation, make a decision, and then move on: a skill set any of us could use in just about any aspect of our lives.

Think about the last time you visited Google.com. You arrived at a page that's incredibly simple. There's that colorful logo in the middle and the box where you type in your search term. There are a few other links on the page, but they're small enough that you don't even notice them if they're not what you're looking for.

That simplicity is by design. The original Google page was put together by a couple of people who knew very little about HTML (hypertext markup language) and kept things sparse so they wouldn't have to learn. Since then, many temptations to dress up the page and fill it with more e-stuff—news, video, stock tickers, advertisements, and so on—have come along, but Google has stayed the course. The company's director of consumer Web products, Marissa Mayer, put it this way:

GOOGLE HAS THE FUNCTIONALITY of a really complicated Swiss Army knife, but the home page is our way of approaching it closed. It's simple, it's elegant, you can slip it in your pocket, but it's got the great doodad when you need it. A lot of our competitors are like a Swiss Army knife open—and that can be intimidating and occasionally harmful.

When I first read this, I knew what our focus at Frank McKinney & Company would be for the following year and beyond: simplicity, which further solidified my growing belief that my company consider no more than ten big-picture objectives a year, as well as my edict that when you send an e-mail, you need to get the essential message across in the subject line. *You mean that with all you do, Frank, you have no more than ten objectives for any given year?* That's right. While there are hundreds of smaller objectives that are born from the "Big Ten," by constantly focusing on the most important big-picture initiatives, I never lose sight of executing what is truly important. Heck, even as I type this paragraph, under my right hand on my laptop is our Annual Objective Plan for 2008 (figure 10.1, p. 173), right there so I see it every day. Previously, I've said that I don't make plans for myself that look farther than a year ahead; this, too, is the product of a desire to simplify.

I can't emphasize enough that the problem of overthinking comes mostly from fear, primarily the fear of doing something wrong, and the net result can be missed opportunities, plans that never translate into reality, even wrong judgment. Overthinking is the enemy of The Tap. Because your Tap Moments are all about acting on the invitation to be of service to someone else, to share yourself, deliberation kills impulse, and initial impulses are typically correct if heeded. If you spend lots of time fretting about perfection, getting all your facts straight, the ramifications on your family, wondering what will happen if you're wrong, suspecting the one you're thinking about benefitting doesn't really need your help and is inflating the truth, lamenting why someone else can't help them, you make it incredibly difficult to feel The Tap at all.

Often, it seems that God is just waiting for you to say yes, for you to act boldly and put your trust in the power of The Tap. I'm reminded of a woman I know, who I'll call Carmen. In her early thirties, she found out that she wouldn't be able to conceive naturally, and this dealt her

Figure 10.1

Frank McKinney & Company and Caring House Project Foundation "The Beauty of Simplicity" Annual Objective Plan

Objective	Completion Date
1) Grade-school compass approach to marketing, promotion, and sales fully underway	By 6/30
2) Acqua Liana 100 percent complete	By 2/13
3) Host grand unveiling for Acqua Liana	By 2/13
4) Crystalina submitted to DEP	By 3/30
5) Crystalina, commence construction	By 10/1
6) Implement CHPF program of work	By 12/31
7) Hire office assistant for FMC and CHPF	By 1/31
8) Pursue executive apprentice who meets superior standards	Until found or not needed
9) Locate new, longer tenured headquarters	By 6/30
10) Perform quarterly AOP, GSCA, CHPF program of work and semiannual employee reviews	3/31, 6/30, 9/30, 12/31
Notes:	

such an emotional blow that she didn't even want to consider any of the options that were open to her. She didn't want to try some other method and fail; it was as if she'd already experienced the death of a child, and each failure or denial would, to her, seem like another death. She simply wasn't ready to face the possibility that whatever she tried next wouldn't work out. Her husband was devastated, too, so they decided together that they'd enjoy other people's children. They'd be a wonderful aunt and uncle; they'd be godparents to many kids; they'd make a family of each other.

When Carmen turned forty, she attended the baptism of one of her godchildren. As she stood in the pulpit with little Emily in her arms for pictures, she could feel the tears forming behind her eyes. *I'll never do this with a child of my own,* she thought. She smiled for the cameras anyway, hiding her pain.

In the week that followed, her sorrow stayed with her. She confided in a friend who wisely asked her, "Carm, what if you just decided to let God take care of this one?"

"But it's too late now," she responded. In the intervening years, Carmen had undergone surgery on her uterus to remove a tumor that had reached, ironically, the size of a six-month-old fetus—and now there was no way she could carry a child. Carmen also knew how long it takes to adopt a child, sometimes up to ten years. Surrogacy was out, too, because it seemed way too complicated.

Again, her friend urged her, "Carm, can't you pray about this and let God figure it out instead of you? And then if something comes up, all you have to do is look into it."

Carmen agreed, although she didn't really believe anything could happen. She did allow some corner of her heart to hope, though. And when she was driving home from work one afternoon, God tapped two words into her head: *foster parent*. Perplexed, Carmen made a mental note to look up foster parenting online when she got home. She didn't know much about "fostering," but she was drawn to that word: *parent*.

In case you don't know, I'll share with you what Carmen shared with me: More than half a million children are in foster care in the United States. They've been removed from their original homes because neither their parents nor relatives are able to care for them. Most come into foster care through Child Protective Services; some are returned to their original homes when the parents are better able to provide a safe environment, while others are permanently removed from their birth parents' care and are then available for adoption. These are called "waiting children," because they await the arrival of a forever family and a permanent home.

So becoming a foster parent was a way to bring a child into their home, either for the short or long term. Carmen and her husband could offer shelter to a little one who needed their love, protection, and care. Carmen talked with Harry about it, and he came on board. He wanted to be a dad as much as Carmen wanted to be a mom. She visited the local social services agency for information, and they signed up for the required parenting courses. Together, they decided to request that the child placed with them be between zero and three years old.

"I have to caution you," the social worker said, "that children this young are not readily available. You may have to wait awhile, maybe several months after your training is done. And even if a child becomes available for adoption, it isn't guaranteed that you'll make it to the finish line together. There are lots of things that can happen, and you have to be prepared for heartache."

Several months! That sounded like no time at all. And Carmen finally felt strong enough to deal with the loss of a child if it came to that. Besides, even if a child were returned to the original home, then that would mean they'd helped not just one child, but his or her birth parents, too. She and Harry would be patient and lean on each other for support, and they'd leave this in God's hands. As it turned out, though, they didn't have to wait at all. A four-week-old girl, Ella, was placed with them long before they expected it, about two weeks before they were done with the parenting course. A year and a half later, Ella's adoption was final, just one month after Carmen's pastor baptized the baby in their church.

Carmen was clearly longing for more, for an enlarged territory in her own family. God answered that prayer with a powerful tap that led her and Harry to adopt a child. If you asked Carmen about this tap, she would tell you that there were enormous blessings she never could have imagined that came with this new territory. If I were to record all that she believes came as a direct result of this one Tap Moment, I'd be writing another book, and that's not an exaggeration. (Maybe someday she'll write her own.) So here's what I want to ask you: What would happen if you decided that you didn't always have to completely figure things out? What if you were willing to make intelligent, informed, but *quick* decisions about the most important parts of your life? What if you were to decide to put your trust in the power of The Tap, think fast, and then act faster?

Your Chapter 10 *Tap* Moments

- Today, choose one thing that you can simplify and stream-line. Consider the company you work for or own; think about your family, your church, your community.

- Remember, God is just waiting for you to say yes, for you to act boldly and put your trust in the power of The Tap. Is there an area of your life that you've been overthinking? Take a moment now to reflect on whether you actually have everything you need to make a decision right now.

- If you were to put together your "life's constitution," and could only include ten initiatives, what would they be?

- What are you overcontemplating? Are you seeking a long, drawn-out no, where a fast yes would be better?

Part Three

Break Through with The Tap Dance!

I hope you've progressed slowly to where you are now, the final section of *The Tap*. In the final chapters of this book, you'll get an inside look at the very real details of leading a tapped life, from the unexpected difficulties to the unanticipated leaps in enlightenment. In "Often Happy, Never Satisfied," you'll start by examining your own ego, which can be a powerful accelerator of your growth or put the brakes on, causing you to skid out of control. I share my own struggles with this and also the more common and debilitating condition, *ego flatline*—and what you can do to either bolster or temper your own sense of self if you need it.

Because most people invest a sizable amount of time, energy, and talent in their work lives, "Doing the Opposite Attracts" brings us into the heart of the business world, where the contrarian approach has served me so well. You'll see how The Tap calls you to turn the tables on so-called common wisdom in business dealings and how you can apply what you believe and what you've learned in this book to your business philosophy and practices, whether you own a company, work in one, serve in the social sector, or run your own home. I bust the usual myths, which I call traps, and show you how they can be turned inside out to create meaningful taps instead.

Living a tapped life involves personal growth and an evolving set of motivations and actions. So far, I've observed seven stages or phases of what I call "The Eternal, Upward Spiral," that one can easily progress through. Anyone can move from insensitivity at the bottom to its complete opposite at the top: eager anticipation and ability to create Tap Moments, which is the high-spirited "tap dance." It's actually very easy to go from where you are right now to Stage Seven, and I'll show you how to break through to the highest levels in a relatively short period of time.

As you ascend that spiral, things can start moving very fast. In my experience, The Tap starts an evolutionary process that proves to be quite revolutionary in your life, and the rate of ascent can sometimes be dizzying. In "Strap Yourself In: Prepare for the Rapid Rate of Ascent," you'll see how land mines are part of the territory, how success can give you greater access to the very things that could obliterate it, and what steps you must take to guard against taking a painful fall.

The last chapter, "The White Line from Hell to Heaven," asks you to take a serious look at how committed you are to living with The Tap. It shows you that what's required isn't all that demanding. This book began by acknowledging that we all want more of something, and that this desire is probably what caused you to start reading. As you reach the end, we come back to that "more" and ask some critical questions: How badly do you want it? Are you willing to do what it takes?

We've come full circle: the beginning is the end . . . *From those to whom much has been given, much will be expected.*

Eleven

OFTEN HAPPY, SELDOM SATISFIED

MANY WHO DON'T KNOW me well perceive me as having a big ego, and it's not a compliment if they say so. I'm often portrayed in the press as self-serving, self-promoting, and egomaniacal. When I recently read those adjectives attached to my name for the umpteenth time in an article in a national paper, the string of words seemed barbed. Even after all of these years, and countless similar references, it still hurts. But then it made me chuckle and say to myself, *I guess there are aspects of the media that will never change. Besides, what's so wrong with those things?* They're solid practices for succeeding in the business of life, so I'll own them, except the egomania part, which is overstated. I am self-serving and self-promoting (I also spend a considerable amount of time "other-serving" and "other-promoting"), and I do have a *healthy* ego.

Heck, we sell a Frank McKinney action figure (take note: we don't call it a "doll") on our website with the hefty price tag of $250. Most people would think that's pretty egotistical, right? First, to have the mini-me at all, and second, to charge so much for it. But if you read the not-so-fine print describing it and its colorful wardrobe, you see that all proceeds benefit the Caring House Project Foundation. I think the whole thing is pretty funny—but I take it very seriously that the money we raise helps build self-sustaining villages for the poor. To date we have sold hundreds of Frank McKinney action figures to benefit hundreds of people. If some folks don't get the joke and don't understand, that's okay. I know what I am. I know who I am. I know why I'm here and, most important of all, who makes it all possible. If that's a big ego, I'm hugely grateful for it.

All of us, at some point in our lives, stop getting the accolades and affirmations we received as children. There comes a time when you've got to start patting yourself on the head and tooting your own horn. There's no harm in that, and I can guarantee there's plenty of good. This is how we continue to grow, both personally and professionally. Just as when we were little, and the encouragement we got for attempting the first step urged us on to the next and the next, when we're adults, we need to become our own cheering section to hearten ourselves to keep moving in the right direction, toward greater and greater things.

Bottom line: You need your ego. It's only three letters, not four. You can say it in polite company. Ego isn't about growing a head so big you can't fit through the doorway. **A healthy, balanced ego is actually a**

necessary asset if you want to feel and act on The Tap. In the pages ahead, you'll see what creates an ego that moves you toward and through your Tap Moments, and the traps that can pull you out of balance. I'll own up to some of my own mistakes and share with you what I've learned from them.

Two Sides of the Coin

WHAT ABOUT THAT EXPRESSION, *healthy ego?* Is it an oxymoron, a contradiction in terms? No, it's not. Out-of-balance egos, on the other hand, are just plain moronic.

True egomania and its extreme opposite, self-deprecation, do nobody any good. You can watch the former on the news regularly, the fifteen-minutes-of-famers trying to squeeze out an extra five or ten in the spotlight. Usually, *egomania* refers to narcissism, being so in love with yourself, so consumed with getting your own needs and desires fulfilled, that you can't think of anything or anyone else. You can find all kinds of unsavory and ridiculous stories of egomania in the headlines pretty often. (Follow politics, religion, sports, business or industry news and you get a steady diet of this stuff.) At the other end of the spectrum, you have those whose egos are on life support and whose stumbles get less attention. They don't seek the limelight—"Who, me? Nobody'd be interested in me"—so their tragedies are considerably more private. But let's not kid ourselves: Just because they don't show up on the nightly news, that doesn't mean they're any less potentially damaging than the egomaniac's blunders.

Can you see how both egomania and ego-flatline could get in the way of your Tap Moments? If you were completely self-absorbed, it would be hard to see your way to some kind of meaningful service. You could easily walk all over people without thinking twice about it. On the other hand, if you didn't believe in yourself and your power to make a difference in someone else's life, how would you ever get up off the couch and try? You could easily become accustomed to the role of doormat, even believe you're destined always to be under someone else's boot. **To lead a tapped life, you need to strive for balance, a healthy midpoint between those two extremes.**

When I extol the virtues of a healthy, balanced ego, I'm talking about several complementary aspects of personality:

- Self-respect and humility
- Self-interest and social responsibility (stewardship)
- Self-esteem and compassion

With all of these in full bloom together, they offset each other, creating self-confidence and the will to do well for yourself and those around you, to use your successes to benefit others, too. **That's the essence of The Tap: self concerns tied to social concerns.** Yet balancing the ego is like any balancing act. You're wobbly at times, occasionally perfectly poised, and sometimes you fall flat on your back. It doesn't matter what level of success you've achieved; this is one of the most difficult endeavors any person attempts.

My observations are based on my own tightrope walk—and I'm still on the line. The title of this chapter, "Often Happy, Seldom Satisfied," reflects a personal evolution that's come from my own struggles. Once upon a time, my motto and worldview was "Often Happy, *Never* Satisfied," which tended to frustrate and burn out some of the people around me, and it contributed to a level of tension and regular dissatisfaction that couldn't have been good for my emotional well-being.

There's no denying that this outlook also produced many unparalleled successes. It drove me toward excellence, especially in my profession. At this stage of my life, though, I continue to work to shed the last part of my old motto, the "never satisfied" part, which lays the traps of perfectionism and ambition that can alienate those around me. Only in the last few years have I truly become aware that there may be other, better ways of viewing and doing business now. One of my wake-up calls came from my uncle, who'd been working with me on one of our estates, when he phoned me *(tap!)* from his sick bed to try to get through to me: "Frank, I gave you my left testicle through all this, and you still want more!" He hadn't literally, but I knew what he meant. "I'm laid up here in the hospital with diverticulitis because I can't eat, and the job environment frequently stresses me out. I've been pushed beyond the breaking point."

That part was unexaggerated.

No doubt my uncle stayed in business with me longer than someone else might have because of family loyalty. Indeed, many other fine people have more readily decided to leave and find other work. Some have left my company in tears *(tap!)*, saying, "It's never good enough for you! You're too hard to please." When I visit with former employees, they usually thank me for an incredible opportunity, and I'm humbled when they report *(tap!)* that I was an impossible boss.

It would be easy for me to dismiss these Tap Moments, tell myself that some people just can't hack it, and keep going on in my same old way. Because I'm aware of The Tap, though, I'm doing my best to pay attention and heed the warning signs. Experiences and remarks like these *(tap, tap, tap!)* have caused me to examine my way of managing people and my hard-charging business persona: *Were there occasions when I could have done things differently and had a more desirable outcome? How will I make better, more conscientious choices in the future?*

My management style continues to be demanding, yet I'm learning to temper my drive with compassion. I'm evolving into what I fondly call the *benevolent dictator,* or an *enlightened absolutist.* In other words, my dictatorial, "what I say goes" nature is still present, but I also consciously focus on taking other people's needs, desires, and limits into account. I do my best to use my power responsibly.

Company-wide standards remain steadfast. Without fail, for example, we still fold the ends of the last sheet on a toilet paper roll into a diamond tip and do a white-glove treatment before we ever show a client one of our estates—and *every* time we show one of the estates—plus attend to hundreds of details, which you'd be astonished to learn, before, during, and after an estate is ready for sale. I still require that, whenever there's a hitch with a project, my staff must bring me proposed solutions instead of presenting problems. That's what we call The Frank McKinney Way. Today, though, I don't drive people as hard as I used to, or as hard as I work myself, nor do I expect them to be as emotionally invested as I am in our projects. They have other priorities in their lives that are just as important to them as my business initiatives are to me, and as long as they're able to perform up to my standards, which are always astronomically high, that has to be enough.

I freely confess I'm still developing in this area: I'm short on compliments, so in my office, kudos are few and far between, and they usually come after some small effort that's extraordinary in my view, like the time Lori saved us $20 a month by bidding out the portable toilet service. Nilsa's much better than I am at acknowledging people for their heart and hard work, while I still tend to focus on results. People regularly get frustrated with my insistence on throwing away the rulebook in all kinds of situations. I have more patience than I used to for people who don't perform according to my expectations—but it's still mighty short—and I show little empathy in sending them on their way.

Do you see any of yourself in this unflattering portrait of me? Does this wake you up to some practices in your own life that may be dictatorial without the benevolence, or absolute without the enlightenment? Don't just think about business. Parents often behave in these ways with children, just as coaches do with teams, even spiritual leaders with congregations—all kinds of leaders in all kinds of situations can fall into the same traps I have. Which ones are you willing to take a closer look at?

Or perhaps you see your opposite here, someone you can't imagine being, much less working for. What does that say about you, for good or ill, that you let people off the hook if they don't live up to your standards, or that you make other people's feelings more important than your own? What can you learn about yourself by noticing that it makes you uncomfortable to imagine running or working in an office like mine?

Whether you identify with me or find my ways completely foreign, can you also see how an ego that's out of balance in either direction might blind you to The Tap? Realize, too, that self-awareness—an acknowledgment of your own ego strengths and shortfalls—can help you bring your Tap Moments back into sharp focus. So take a look at how your ego affects your ability to truly succeed, not just in business, but in the business of life. Just as with the risk tolerance continuum you read about earlier in this book, you can gauge where you are on the spectrum from a deflated ego ("I'm not as good as everyone else") to a healthy ego (with a grounded perspective on your own strengths and weaknesses) to an inflated ego ("I'm more important than everyone else").

Ego Continuum

Deflated ⟷ *Healthy* ⟷ *Inflated*

Celebrate Each Humble Victory as a Triumphant Achievement

THROUGHOUT THIS CHAPTER, I've been revealing the pitfalls of an ego that tends toward the inflated end of the spectrum. But what are the traps of the other side? The one that's most difficult to shake is the idea that because you're somehow insignificant or imperfect or unworthy or otherwise "less than," your actions don't matter. So why try? The heavy fog that descends over the psyche when the ego's out of balance in this way can be completely stifling. I imagine that those people I mentioned in the beginning of this book, the ones Tom and I watched driving on the highway with that look of resignation, exhaustion, and desperation, must have felt this way.

There's no study I've found to support this, but I have a hunch that more people tend toward the ego-flatline side of the spectrum than the other. As Henry David Thoreau wrote, "The mass of men lead lives of quiet desperation." **This is a total rejection of the idea that we can all be tapped, that each of us can be responsible stewards of immense blessings if we choose to be,** that everyone has many opportunities to be special in that way. It's a denial of the power of Tap Moments to transform an individual through simple acts. The sinking self-confidence of a deflated ego drags you under, keeping you anchored to the bottom of a small, dark, murky territory that is the untapped life. In this state, you might start thinking that God's "best" blessings are for everyone but you, and you should feel lucky just to get any scraps that fall your way.

It's depressing and demoralizing, and no wonder people who believe this way feel empty and sorry for themselves, unable to recognize a Tap Moment even when it comes slamming through the door like a SWAT team.

How do you end such a vicious cycle of doubt?

One way is to go forward with courage, even if you don't think The Tap will ever work for you. Remember Carmen, who adopted a child after thinking she'd never be a mom. All it took was an act of *willingness,* a demonstration of *interest,* and the solution was presented to her. Then she had to move forward with courage. Was it completely risk-free? No, it wasn't. Later in this book, I'll share the story of another woman in a similar situation who was tapped to make an almost unimaginable personal sacrifice for her child. These circumstances aren't without their potential for pain, for loss or disillusionment or any other kind of heartache. But you can't let the downside stop you from moving forward. You've already read about risk tolerance and its relationship to The Tap. Clearly, it also has intimate ties to your self-confidence. Each time you attempt something and learn from it, you strengthen your risk tolerance and build your self-confidence. Each humble victory leads to greater and greater accomplishments. Courage—acting in spite of your fear—is like a light: It doesn't take much of a flame to dispel the darkness. One simple, courageous act, one brave moment, teaches you that what you do *does* make a difference and that there's no such thing as a powerless person. It nurses the ego, restoring it to glowing health.

The Body Shop founder Anita Roddick once said, "If you think you're too small to have an impact, try going to bed with a mosquito in the room." If you're experiencing self-doubt and still hanging onto the notion that The Tap and its inherent blessings are only for other people, now's your chance to be that mosquito in the room. Go on: Take a bite and draw a little.

So let's say you've prayed for better health, for example, and you've been tapped for the first time to start teaching a free exercise class for senior citizens. Someone asked you to lead it, and you said yes, or else you just thought it up on your own. Actually following through on that—arranging for a place to do it, getting the word out, selecting the music and planning the class, lacing up your shoes, and showing up at the appointed hour—that's your extremely brave act for the moment. You show up, in spite of any doubts you have about your ability, or if anyone will come, or if they'll like what you do. Now this is an incredibly important part of confidence building: When even one person shows up to work out with you, *you must celebrate that humble victory as a triumphant achievement.* Reward yourself as if you'd just taught a master's class to a studio full of one hundred people! You might crack open a bottle of champagne with some friends, or treat yourself to a sports massage, or take your one student out to dinner at a nice restaurant.

Reflecting on each of the little steps, those humble victories, leads to another and then another, until you're at the top of your game and a long way from where you started. Back in August of 2006, I had a landmark month: We sold all our inventory, three large oceanfront mansions, in a thirty-day period, for $88 million. It was a crazy, unbelievable run of accomplishments, and it left my head spinning. When I sat down to collect my thoughts, you know what was on my mind? All the deals I'd done before, starting with the first house that yielded a modest $7,000 in profit. That was some of the most exciting money I'd ever made, because it showed me I could do it.

That first sale and every other one after it had led me to the spectacular earnings of my multimillion-dollar, three-property windfall month. Keep in mind that this was now twenty years later! As I've said before, I didn't go straight from the $50,000 fixer-upper in a distressed neighborhood to the oceanfront estates that now command eight and nine figures. There were many steps, and many taps, from there to here, which is precisely my point: With each humble victory comes increased self-confidence and the courage to take your next step, to respond to your *next* Tap Moment.

In this book, you've read about all kinds of Tap Moments, from Julio Diaz's encounter with a would-be mugger; to Bill Gates and Bono acting together to change world health; to Bob, whose loss of a job turned into a golden opportunity; to Doug, who took a huge leap of faith financially and was rewarded several times over; to the eighty-some-year-old woman in South Africa who was carried to the polling place to cast her first ballot and helped make history; to the young man for whom a national tragedy became a time to summon the courage to stand up for a man he admired; to a teacher who pays attention to her students' home lives and supports them however she can; to Carmen, who broke through her fear and adopted a child; to the experiences I've shared with you from my own life of being tapped in so many large and small ways. If you'd like to see a complete list of *all* the Tap Moments captured in these pages, turn to the index in the back of the book, or visit The-Tap.com and click on the "Share Your Tap Moments" link to see current stories shared by others from around the world. You'll be struck by the diversity of people and ways in which they've been tapped. Can a person look at this list and still think that The Tap is reserved for a select few? It's certainly possible, though at this point, dear reader, I hope you're not tempted to dismiss how great a force The Tap can be, nor how great a force it is in your own life right now.

YOUR CHAPTER 11 *Tap* MOMENTS

- How does your ego hinder or help your professional life?

- How does your ego affect your relationships at home and at work?

- How does your ego attune you to The Tap, or else make you numb to it?

- What areas of your ego need to be developed: self-respect, self-interest, or self-esteem—or humility, social responsibility (stewardship), and compassion?

- Would you say you are closer to "Often Happy, Never Satisfied" or "Often Satisfied, Never Happy"?

- Set aside fifteen minutes to brainstorm a list of Tap Moments, big and small, from your own life. Enlist a spouse, significant other, or close friend to help you recall. I promise this will be even more inspiring than the list you'll find in the back of this book or at The-Tap.com. To prompt your list, ask yourself, *At what times in my life have I been called to something greater? When have I acted on The Tap, and when have I dismissed it? How can I be even more aware of the opportunities that surround me every day to use the blessings I've already received to assist someone else?* Once you're finished with the list, post it on your refrigerator or in some conspicuous place to remind you of the power of The Tap. Please consider sharing your stories of your Tap Moments by visiting The-Tap.com, where we will publically share your words with others who are seeking encouragement and enlightenment from your experiences.

Twelve

DOING THE OPPOSITE
ATTRACTS

IT'S NOT PERSONAL—it's just business. Win-win is the name of the game. Take the power position at the bargaining table. Profit is king. Faith and fortune don't mix.

That's business as usual, isn't it? Everyone has heard these platitudes, and so many have fallen into lockstep with their tired march across the corporate landscape. In my experience, though, going a completely opposite direction—being the contrarian, the maverick, the so-called paradoxicologist—has led to *better* business, *more* business, and long-term professional relationships. I naturally gravitate to the road less traveled and continue to be thrilled when it pays off. In business, especially, I've been repeatedly rewarded for going my own way.

Whether you're an entrepreneur, intrapreneur, employee, or someone who works outside the business world, you can benefit by bucking the system, too. In this chapter, I bust some of the common business myths I consider *traps* and show you how you can apply the principles of The Tap everywhere, from the boardroom to the water cooler.

The Trap: It's Not Personal—It's Just Business

The Tap: Make All Business Personal

THAT SAYING MAKES my skin crawl: "It's not personal—it's just business" gives license to treat some people as less than human, as means to an end. This runs contrary to the central idea of The Tap, which dictates that you treat all people well in every circumstance, including customers and merchants, clients and vendors.

As you go through life attuning yourself to Tap Moments, which almost always come through interaction with someone you know or meet, why would you approach any one person or group of people differently? From the individual who clears your table after you have eaten in a restaurant or cleans the bathroom at a public building or fixes your car to the one who writes your paycheck or sorts your correspondence, you're wise to see every interaction as personal and *not* "just business." Anything else is dehumanizing for everyone involved, and that, of course, includes you. (I'm reminded of this great line from the book *The Go-Giver* by Bob Burg and John David Mann: "You want people skills? Then be a *person*.")

Frank McKinney & Company has a reputation of being a pleasure to buy from and a pleasure to sell to, which I'm sure reflects our commitment to personal relationships. Still, I'm not perfect, and I understand how easy it is to forget to be considerate and kind when you're focused on deliverables or deadlines; it's common to overlook the need for personal connection when you just want to get the job done; it's accepted practice to put your bottom line before the needs of others. Yet, if you seek greater territory—which in business usually means more income, profit, customers or a change in your job status—you now know that you must be a responsible steward of the money, clientele, and job you already have. Realize that whenever you transact business with someone (e.g., you write a check to pay the plumber, you talk to a customer on the phone, you're assigned to a new work team, you ring up a sale), almost every occasion presents opportunities to demonstrate how responsible you are. Tap Moments abound in the business world.

From those to whom much has been entrusted, much will be expected. Making business personal can affect everything from how you decide to compensate employees to whether you participate in water-cooler gossip. It can determine how you approach negotiation, seek a promotion, and assume a leadership position at any level of the organization. If you're attuning yourself to The Tap, then you're called to be a responsible steward in *all* parts of your life, which requires that you translate your spiritual beliefs into practical actions even in the workplace. If one of your objectives is to gain more traction financially, then your supposedly secular workday is the first place to consider infusing with more spirit. Whether you're a stay-at-home mom or a Fortune 500 CEO, it's probably the place where you spend the most time and certainly where you circulate the most money. Why not seek God there, too?

The Trap: "Win-Win Is the Name of the Game" ·

The Tap: Let the Other Person Come Out on Top

FOR MANY PEOPLE, it's as if they have a little angel on one shoulder promoting the virtues of win-win and a devil on the other that pressures them to "win bigger" than the other person. Because of this, "win-win" usually is just a linguistic front for another kind of win-lose deal. Instead of trying to play that game, dancing around and pretending to create a totally equal outcome for both parties, why not play a different game altogether? Why not decide that your goal is for the other person to feel like the winner? It's better business if the other person feels as if he or she has come out with the better end of the deal.

Why? If we're looking strictly at business principles, creating a win for the other person builds customer loyalty and repeat business, two crucial elements of any successful enterprise, whether we're talking about $30 million homes or $30 pairs of shoes. And a "win" is perceived when the other person doesn't have to compromise on what's most important to him or her.

In fact, put yourself in those shoes for a minute. You walk into a store and see a big banner announcing a sale. Right off, you know some of the deal points are set: The prices on the products are reduced, and they're unlikely to be discounted further, so there's no haggling. You do need to negotiate size, comfort, color, style, and any number of other factors. If the person behind the counter is courteous, efficient, and helpful, you could stride out of the shop feeling like you've just gotten a great deal on a pair of shoes you love. You're a winner! If, on the other hand, you walk out of the store feeling as if you've compromised—your shoes don't quite fit, they're not exactly the color you wanted, the person helping you was rude, or you couldn't find a pair on sale (the old bait and switch)—then how likely are you to return to shop there again? Not half as likely as if you walk out feeling you've just won the shoe-buying equivalent of the Grand Slam.

If you take it a step further, and remember that all business is personal and that The Tap calls you to bring your spiritual principles into action with everyone you meet, then you see that helping someone else get exactly what they want, even (or especially) in a business transaction, is its own kind of Tap Moment.

Whenever I'm closing the deal on one of our multimillion-dollar estates, I make it my job to ensure that the buyer has that ultimate experience. After the dust settles, my buyers may wind up scratching their heads, thinking, *What just happened? I thought I was going to stay at the Ritz this winter, but wow! I am so pleased that I now have this beautiful, permanent home on the ocean in Palm Beach. This is like my own private resort . . . I never would have imagined this, much less how fast it all came together!*

When buying property, I work to give my seller the same kind of experience. Because I frequently purchase land from older people, it's important for me to remember that this transaction will probably represent a major life change for them. Most of my sellers have lived in their homes for decades and invested nearly a lifetime of memories and mortgage payments there. So I do my best to provide them with what they need to feel good about selling to me. I've allowed some older couples to stay in the home, even after they've sold it to me, for up to a year rent-free. I've helped a number of people find a new place to live and sent movers over to help them. I do this because I want them to feel that they've gotten a great deal in selling to me. I also do it because, after getting to know these people, I genuinely like them—their business becomes personal to me; they could be my parents or grandparents, or me in a few decades, and their win becomes much more important than my own.

In these dealings, interactions, and transactions, if successful, the other party is so pleased, even euphoric, with the outcome that they *feel* as if they are the only one that matters, kind of a heads-they-win, tails-they-win sensation. Their experience deviates from having to look out for and protect their own interests to one of trust. They don't think about win-win, win-lose, or lose-win—they are so intoxicated with their result that your side of the equation is unimportant. They're so overwhelmed by what they've gotten that they don't care if you've won, lost, or walked out the door in a pink gorilla suit. They're blinded by their happiness.

To put a fine point on it: You've made their win the most important part of the deal.

Of course, you should never agree to terms where you feel as if you've "lost" just to create a win for the other person. You protect and promote your interests privately, but you focus publicly on their interests. In the process, if the other party *feels* superior, yet deep down you are completely satisfied, even euphoric yourself, then this is your quiet victory.

The Trap: "Take the Power Position at the Bargaining Table"

The Tap: Sit in the Other Person's Chair First

To CREATE A win for the other person, you need to know more about what they want than what you want. I can't even tell you, for example, what net amount of money I'd be willing to accept for any of the properties or land we are offering for sale right now. People often think there's some magical number I have in my head, but there isn't. In fact, I can often figure out what the offer will be before I know what I will accept, because I know my market so well. My own number will be based on the peripheral terms associated with the deal: the tenor of the negotiation, inspections, the closing date, the "vibe" of the deal, and so on (to use our shoe analogy again: size, fit, comfort, color). Most people assume any real estate deal, and especially a big one, is just about money, but it's not. There are so many other pieces, tangible and intangible, including my sentiment about how much trouble a potential buyer will be during the one-year warranty period we include with every Frank McKinney & Company estate home. If my commitment is to make this person feel like a winner in every interaction with me, what will that take? If I don't see the possibility of making that happen, there's no way I'll sign on the dotted line, no matter how big a check might be dangling in front of me.

You could also say that I often know more about what the other person wants than *they* do, at least subconsciously. That comes from years of experience, paying attention to buyers and sellers, noting what the other party desires at the particular phase of life they're in, the kinds of relationships they have, the current state of their business, their family concerns, and so on. There are over a hundred layers that speak to me without so many words, informing my choices every step of the way. (If you want more detailed information on specific real estate practices, consider picking up *Burst This! Frank McKinney's Bubble-Proof Real Estate Strategies.* Meanwhile, can you see how all of this parallels many other kinds of business dealings and areas of life?) What will make the other person feel like a winner? Is this someone who needs time to make up his or her mind, or will actions come more on impulse? Will good terms be the piece that tips the scales? Would this person like someone else to attend to every detail? When I ask these questions, I *listen* to the answers. Even if I never get around to asking about something specific, I've learned to read between the lines and know what the other person wants and needs.

How? Part of it can be chalked up to experience, having studied my market for nearly twenty-five years, constantly honing my under-standing. Whether a deal goes through or not, I always find out *why*. Beyond that, I have an unorthodox routine: Prior to any negotiation, I literally sit in the other person's chair. Old-school negotiating tactics say you should only sit in the power position, stay on your side of the desk or take the head of the table, stake your claim there, and don't budge. It's supposed to be intimidating. Yet I find that if I arrive early and sit in the other person's chair, I gain even more insights about them. Everything I've learned from prior meetings, including personality, preferences, background, even body language, helps me imagine I *am* that person and consider what their needs or concerns might be. After I do this exercise, it becomes even clearer to me what I need to do to finalize a deal.

While I don't have a lot of time to read blogs, I did run across something by author Marshall Goldsmith that caught my attention and is worth sharing with you here. He was making a point about how truly successful people are such great listeners. "There's no on-off switch for caring, empathy, and showing respect. It's always on," he wrote.

He also offered this simple way to assess your listening skills: Close your eyes, count to fifty, and try not to let another thought interrupt the count. Can you make it past twenty or thirty without some random notion messing up your concentration? Marshall wrote that this is such a useful exercise to assess your listening skill because, "After all, if you can't listen to yourself (someone you presumably like) as you count to fifty, how will you ever be able to listen to another person?"

Try it yourself and see how far you can get. The first time I did it, I got to forty-one, but then this thought popped into my head: "I'm going to make it to fifty!"

The Trap: "Profit Is King"

The Tap: Create All Kinds of Capital

IN THE LATE 1970s, when Spanish psychiatrist Cristóbal Colón first became the director of a hospital's work therapy program, he did what most people in his position did back then: He gave the mental health patients meaningless tasks to keep their hands busy. (Think summer camp crafts, like pipe-cleaner art and bubblegum-wrapper chains and ceramic ashtrays.) At the time, this was business as usual for psychiatric care, but Cristóbal eventually grew frustrated with it and experienced a Tap Moment. He concluded that this "treatment" fell far short of making any real difference for patients. They needed more than just something to do; like anyone else, they would benefit from a sense of dignity and purpose and pride—they didn't need busywork; they needed real jobs.

So that's what he decided to create for them. Like the visionary explorer with whom he shares a name (Christopher Columbus is the English version), he set out into uncharted waters. He sought a loan and started a dairy farm in Cataluña. (Oh, I would have loved to have been a fly on the loan officer's wall that day. Translation: "Hi, I'm a psychiatrist and want to start a farm. No, not a funny farm. I want to buy cows. My name? Christopher Columbus.")

Since 1982, La Fageda has captured the third-largest market share for yogurt in its area. It rakes in over $10 million a year, but Cristóbal has never made profit his sole motive for operations. He has more of a "soul" motive: It has always been driven by a desire to create social capital, to provide a real chance for mental health patients to make a better life for themselves. Workers get paid well, many live on site, and there is a fully staffed mental health facility that serves the working population on the farm. Psychiatric patients are referred by governmental agencies, employed by the dairy farm, and undergo treatment there with the ultimate objective of being reintegrated into society.

While profit is still a part of the equation—it allows La Fageda to be self-sustaining without donors—it's hardly king.

Similar ambitions led Bangladeshi banker and economist Muhammad Yunus to found Grameen Bank, renowned for its successful establishment of microlending, or issuing small loans, some of which are less than the cash you carry in your wallet. Before he established the bank, Muhammad had made his first loan out of his own pocket—*tap!*—to a collective of forty-two women who made bamboo furniture and lived in a small village. He gave them $27, and they turned a profit of .84 on the goods they made and sold with the loan. That's a return of 3.1 percent, or two cents per person, which, at first glance, may sound insignificant. It was anything but. Without the microcredit, these women would have had to borrow at usurious rates to buy the bamboo they needed—they were too poor for a traditional bank loan—and they would have yielded no financial return and so had no incentive to ply their trade. Yet with the small loan, Muhammad and the women launched a profit center for the village, banking social return at the same time. Today, Grameen continues to operate on the principle that tiny loans made at reasonable rates are tools for economic and social development among the poorest people, and the bank pours its profits back out into communities in the form of new loans. Grameen and Muhammad Yunus shared the Nobel Peace Prize in 2006 for their efforts to address poverty issues and bring about needed change "from below."

Let it be known that Muhammad is one of my living heroes, yet he provides just one example of the many, many ventures that put the highest value on social returns. They're cropping up all over the world, from the traditional charities like my own Caring House Project Foundation, to the hybrid nonprofits that blend revenue generation with philanthropy, to the for-profit social business ventures like La Fageda.

It may seem like an odd comparison, but Muhammad, Cristóbal, and the legions of compassionate capitalists put me in mind of the first verse of an old Rush song, "Closer to the Heart":

AND THE MEN [PEOPLE] who hold high places
Must be the ones who start
To mold a new reality
Closer to the heart

What can you learn from these new social business models, and what do they have to do with The Tap? Something you already know but most common business practices belie: Financial profit is important, but it's not most important. Tapping your financial resources can start to take on a whole new meaning when you start thinking about social enhancement, social returns, social capital—molding a new reality that's closer to the heart. In other words, creating ways that business can have an impact, bettering people's lives and the world in which we live. This defines compassionate capitalism, the commitment to use, make, and deliver products and services in such a way that it serves both the worker and the consumer, and carries the torch for transformational social or environmental change. It goes by another, older name, too: responsible stewardship.

You may be thinking that this all sounds pretty high-minded and far-reaching, but let me ask you something: Are there opportunities for you to impact the environment (either the social climate or the physical surroundings) where you work right now? If you look around, I'm sure you'll find lots of ways to make an impact. As we complete the world's largest and most opulent certified "green" homes, I've been delighted to hear that many of our employees have taken it all to heart. Big, burly construction workers have told me that they're carpooling in compact cars to cut down on emissions. Escalating gas prices probably helped convince them, but they say it's more about taking care of the environment. They have even gone so far as strategically placing bins around the site to hold soda cans for recycling. In the twenty-plus years I've been in the business, I've never witnessed such transformational behavior.

How about you? Could you set the tone for more constructive conversation at the water cooler, set up a recycling bin near the copier or printer, encourage carpooling, organize a team to raise funds for a noble cause, take up a nonholiday toy drive—bring some of The Tap spirit into your workplace? When you stop focusing solely on the bottom line, and instead look to bring some soul into the workplace, you can create all kinds of capital that enhance the business, the people it serves and who serve it, as well as the world around us.

The Trap: "Faith and Fortune Don't Mix"

The Tap: Bring God into the Boardroom

DOES POLITICAL CORRECTNESS dictate that we act as if God doesn't exist in our nine-to-five? I don't want to get into the whole debate about when and where and whether you should pray in public, but I do want to address this idea that you should (or could) separate your spiritual life from your professional life.

Let me just lay it on the line: You can't. I tried when I was younger, and it didn't work. You can pretend that your beliefs about God have no bearing on your workday or your business dealings . . . you can behave as if God matters only when you're in a place of worship or your own home, but there's a word for this: *hypocrisy*. Think of it as the spiritual equivalent of a split personality. It damns you to a kind of hell in the here and now. If you take a moment to reflect on what it really means to compartmentalize God, to stash your spirit away in a corner every day but Sunday, you realize that it leads to only one conclusion: a fractured and even tortured sense of self. If you have a conscience, it eventually makes you feel guilty and empty and lost.

Choosing to live with greater integrity, meaning that your beliefs and your actions line up as much as possible, doesn't necessarily create a huge external change, although it can. You don't have to start wearing a robe to work, and you don't have to stand on the street corner during your lunch hour and broadcast religious doctrine. (Although, I have to tell you, those people with messages on signs and sandwich boards aren't usually as crazy as they seem. I stop to talk with people who do this, and I'm always intrigued to find out how many of them are clear-headed and perfectly sane. They just have incredible conviction about their beliefs, and I have to respect that.) Nor do you need to indoctrinate your coworkers or insist that everyone conform to your concept of God and godliness. I'm sure there will be plenty of people who will see this book and criticize me for not going far enough, or for not using my influence to give it the slant they would have liked to see. No, that's just not my style. There's a profound difference between being a devoted spiritual person, committed to your own beliefs and practices, and treating other people as if their beliefs and practices are stupid or wrong. The line dividing those two positions is so incredibly wide that I'm surprised how many people still trip over it constantly. However, just to be plain about it: What I'm encouraging is that you allow your spiritual life to inform your practical actions, that you don't foist your beliefs on other people, but that you don't hide them, either.

I realize I may be preaching to the choir; if you've read this far, you're probably already infusing your secular life with the sacred. But I wonder if you could take it even further. Once you commit yourself to feeling and following The Tap, God's hand in all aspects of your life becomes incredibly obvious, because Tap Moments come at all places and times. God doesn't respect the boundaries we fabricate to separate the spiritual and the secular. As I've said a few times already, God is just as likely to tap you in the 7-Eleven or Target as on some magnificent hilltop. From what I've observed, God couldn't care less about the scenery, and Tap Moments come from the most unlikely corners.

It's easy to start thinking that you're doing your part, that you've carved out your niche and what you're already doing to share with others is "enough." Yet I'm regularly humbled by these "out-of-nowhere" Tap Moments. When Hurricane Katrina devastated the southern coast of the United States, it was an unexpected call to service that led me to organize a relief effort then drive to the affected areas in one of two 24-foot cargo trucks the Caring House Project Foundation and donors filled with pallets of essentials. It's like the almost weekly taps that can appear in the form of a family living out of the back of their car, who have somehow found their way to us, and we drop everything we're doing to see if we can have them sleeping comfortably in a hotel the very same night the need comes to our attention.

A recent example of a Tap Moment that came out of nowhere is one I wrote about in an earlier chapter: the million-meal campaign for Haiti during the first peak of the world food crisis. This came at a time when I was deeply involved with the Caring House Project Foundation's already aggressive program of work, also consumed with writing three books (one you hold in your hand), designing a new $30 million home, finishing another $29 million home, travelling to give speeches, and training for Badwater. You could say that I had a lot going on, but I was clearly and loudly tapped to help out. Our foundation charter has nothing to do with emergency hunger relief, but it was obviously the right thing to do. I could have listened to my own excuses: "Somebody else can handle that," "I have too much going on," "That's not what I do." (Sound familiar?) I could have tried to divorce what was obviously a spiritual imperative from the practical activities of my life—but I didn't.

You'll see why, especially, after you read the next chapter and learn about Stage 7 in the upward spiral of The Tap.

For the person who's living a tapped life, there's no on-off switch for spirit. You allow it to infuse your life with the wonder and will of God. You purposefully look for opportunities to *act* in ways that dovetail with your beliefs. You don't allow conventional wisdom, excuses, or the way things have always been done to hold you back. In one breath, you feel The Tap, and in the next, you act.

Your Chapter 12 *Tap* Moments

- If you work outside the home, for the next few days, observe how people behave in the office. Is there some bit of corporate culture you can stand on its head? In what ways can you zig where everyone else is zagging, and make a positive impact in the process?

- Where have you fallen into the trap of treating other people as if it's "just business"? Is there a simple thing you could do to make it more personal? Do you owe anyone an apology or a follow-up call to smooth things over?

- Think about how many opportunities you have to sit in the other person's chair: if you're a parent, you can sit in your child's chair; if you work in an office, you can sit in your coworker's chair, or sit behind your employer's desk, or, if other people work for you, you can sit at their workstations and see what that's like. Choose one person whose chair you'll occupy this week, then do it!

- What opportunities do you see to increase social capital? If you own a business, what can you do to incorporate some of the principles of the social business models?

THE ETERNAL,
UPWARD SPIRAL

WHEN I FIRST STARTED volunteering one hour a week to serve meals for The Caring Kitchen, I didn't understand it as a Tap Moment. All I knew was that I'd worked extremely hard for and experienced incredible rewards, and there were other people who were homeless and hungry. Remember, I had opened up my newspaper and seen myself on one side of the fold, celebrating a record-breaking real estate deal, and the opposite page featured a photo of a man who looked like my twin, eating at a soup kitchen. *Here I am, with my multimillion-dollar properties, in a position many people envy, and able to afford whatever meal I want to eat, and there he is, living on the street and huddled over some food he probably feels lucky to get.* In a word, I felt *guilty* about it, so volunteering was a way to make me feel better about myself and my success. It worked.

My personal evolution continued from there. Eventually, I found new incentives for giving, new ways of looking at my contributions, new levels of commitment and compassion. Throughout my own growth, and in observing other people on their paths of development, I've noticed seven clear stages that I like to imagine as a spiral circling upward. And, like a tornado, the force of the upper levels is what makes a bigger impact on the ground. Yet if you don't look to progress through the stages, the spiral turns into nothing more than a maddening circle. You know, they say the definition of insanity is doing the same thing over and over again, and expecting different results. A stalled spiral is like that, and how often do we seek a solution to our life's problems by taking the same failed approach?

As you read the next few pages, see if you can identify where you are now on this upward spiral. At what stage are you living your life? Be honest with yourself about this, brutally so. Once you're able to identify your current level of development, it lights the way to moving on to the next.

Stage One: Checked Out and Tapped Out

WHEN YOU WERE a toddler, like every other child, you thought that what you needed, what you felt, and what you wanted mattered most. You may have had some vague sense that other people had needs, feelings, and desires, but those things were about as meaningful to you as the furniture in your parents' living room.

Some people grow out of toddlerhood without ever shaking this profound self-absorption. They never learn to share, which any kindergartner will tell you is an important social skill. Or if they have learned about it, they have rejected it as inconvenient, imprudent, or sentimental, like Scrooge in the first few acts of *A Christmas Carol*. Even acknowledging the existence of The Tap is completely outside the realm of possibility—they're numb to the feeling and blind to the blessings. This stage is like a black hole of the soul, consuming and consumed with the "I." It produces a spiritually blank stare, as a person can see the world around him or her, but none of it really registers. It's a state of social unconsciousness, a nearly complete lack of awareness or care for other people. The spiral has yet to rotate, and if it does turn, it revolves around the "I."

It's not that people at Stage One don't ever come in contact with reality, but it just does not compute. As an adult, it's nearly impossible not to bump up against the harshness of our world. Some people experience lives that are dire and scary and awful, and they're featured everywhere in the media, while clear signs of poverty and distress are present even in the smallest towns. At Stage One, these gritty facts of life are dismissed as unrelated to the all-important, insatiable, insensitive "I."

The unconscious Stage-One response to The Tap: *See ya. I wouldn't want to be ya.*

I'd also go as far as stating that much sin occurs in Stage One.

Stage Two: Tap Roots

THE SEEDS OF awareness and compassion are planted when the world around you starts to take some shape and meaning for you. You see the news, and the images of other people's suffering stick somewhere in your consciousness. You hear about a neighbor's troubles, and you find yourself being mildly concerned. You get word that your friend has experienced a real letdown, and you briefly feel sorry for that person.

Yet at this stage, you're still unwilling to do anything about it. In fact, you attempt to shut off your awareness because it makes you uncomfortable. You change the channel. You delete the e-mail. You choose to gossip about the need, instead of really processing it. You don't answer the phone when you see a familiar number on caller I.D. You move on, quickly. Your feeling is "I can't do anything about it," or else "I don't want to do anything about it." You have your own stuff to deal with, and it's way more important than anything else. If you spent time with someone else, who would take care of your needs? If you gave somebody money, then there'd be less for you, right? You might think, *That charity stuff is for do-gooders and idealists. I don't have the time or the money or the inclination to get involved. I have to take care of me.*

Something is starting to pull at you—you're in the earliest phase of being sensitized to The Tap—but it feels like an unwanted and uninvited responsibility. Giving and sharing sound like saccharine ideas, and when you do engage in these activities, it's begrudgingly. Buying someone a holiday or birthday gift is an irritating obligation. In this stage, the pie is only so big, and you want to hang onto your piece. You need to evaluate what you can afford to do and weigh that against what you might get in return.

The still-unconscious Stage-Two response to The Tap: *Don't even go there; I don't have the time, the money, or the desire.* Here again, sin abounds.

Stage Three: Tap Shoes

BETWEEN STAGE TWO and Stage Three is the threshold of *action*. The guilt associated with what you can't avoid knowing now gets heavy enough that you're ready to do something about it. So you pull on your "tap shoes" and start shuffling along. They feel awkward and a little uncomfortable. They make more noise than you expected, and you might find that embarrassing. You're not dancing yet, but you're up and moving.

There's a sense of social pressure to give something back. There's a perceived expectation that you'll at least behave as if you're grateful and generous. So you give sparingly because you think you have to give *something*. Your contributions are reluctant. You give the leftovers and hand-me-downs in your life, the things you don't want and have no excuse to hang onto. As an usher in my church, I can spot those who are at Stage Three not by how much they put in the offering, but by the manner in which they do it: Either they grumble and hang their head or bury a multifolded bill, palms down so that the denomination can't be seen, deep into the collection basket. It's a chore to them, like taking out the garbage or emptying the dishwasher.

The emerging awareness of Stage Three creates this response to The Tap: *What's the least I can do? Whatever it is, I'm sure it's all I can do, so don't ask me for more.*

Stage Four: Tap Show

MUCH OF THIS stage is about image, both your self-image and what you think is socially acceptable and necessary. You make contributions to causes that will publish your name (if they have different levels of benefactors, you give the minimum amount to get you into a desired category). You exaggerate your involvement in volunteer work or wear your efforts like a badge. You talk about what you do for others with a tone of reverence, as if you're surprised at your own good will. Individuals and organizations who are the recipients of your generosity are viewed as "those people."

Giving makes you feel better about yourself and, you imagine, makes you look good to your peers. You want to be perceived as always making the grand gesture, so you tend not to respond to the "small" Tap Moments yet. Opportunities to do simple kindnesses pass you by without being recognized. If it doesn't feather your nest, it's not worth your attention.

The Stage-Four response to The Tap: *How will this make me look? Someone better be watching as I share, or I will wait until they are to give.*

Stage Five: Tapping the Scales

THIS IS THE stage I was experiencing when I was looking at the paper that day, eyeing "myself" on both sides of the fold. Those photographs hit me with a need to restore some social balance; they triggered my success guilt and pushed me over the edge to really identify with the idea that "There, but for the grace of God, go I." In that moment, I got it: This man who looked like me and I were one and the same. I felt the need to tip the scales, to *tap* the scales, into a new balance.

At this stage, you tend to give when things are good. You do it because giving is more comfortable when you feel comfortable yourself, and it seems like the right thing to do. *I just hit that home run and landed a big client. It's okay to give now.* But it's somewhat self-limiting, in that whenever you perceive that something's not going as well, the first place you cut corners is in your response to Tap Moments. *Hmmm, it's just not a good time for me to put myself out there. I don't have as much (fill in the blank: time, money, energy, etc.) as I'd like to, so I'm going to have to say no for now.* You're a fair-weather friend to The Tap.

There's a certain superstition that starts to creep in, too: *If things are going so well for me, I need to do something nice for someone else just to keep the other shoe from dropping.* Responding to Tap Moments seems like a good luck charm, keeping the winds of fate blowing in your favor.

The Stage-Five response to The Tap: *It feels good to give and I'll give when the getting's good!*

Stage Six: Tap Watershed

WHILE STAGE FIVE is a turning point, Stage Six is a real breakout. This quantum leap comes when you train your focus on others, when you begin to truly evolve a social conscience and consciousness. At the same time, the feelings of being good and doing the right thing intensify so that you're willing to feel and follow through on your Tap Moments even when it doesn't seem like the "right time." You're compelled to do it because it gives you such a sense of self-worth and purpose that nothing else can compare. You know this is one of the things you were put here on earth to do: to care for others, to help them whenever you can, to say yes more than no, to make an effort to treat everyone with the utmost respect and compassion. You begin to understand your spiritual highest calling in life, and that without one, even the most profound professional highest calling is rendered shallow and often even meaningless. With frequency, you begin to apply the timeless biblical wisdom, *from those to whom much is entrusted, much will be expected*. You are also entering what I refer to as the early phases of the "Proactive Tap Dance" stage. You begin to seek opportunities to tap rather than waiting for them to present themselves to you.

The Stage-Six response to The Tap: *I feel it, and yes, I will act on it.*

Stage Seven: Fully Tapped In

THIS IS WHERE you want to be, and it is really not that difficult to attain. Responsible stewardship. Highest calling. Purpose. Enlightenment.

Godliness. All of these are part of Stage Seven, when The Tap becomes such a part of who you are, so woven into the fabric of your life, that it's not about your feelings anymore. Sometimes you feel good, and sometimes you feel neutral, and sometimes it feels like a chore to respond to The Tap. You are now sensitized to all of life's Tap Moments, and treat every opportunity with reverence and with great importance, regardless of how it appears. For it is the collection of the actions taken when presented with small Tap opportunities that make the most meaningful difference in the lives of others. Why? Because while the large Tap Moments are wonderful, smaller, almost daily taps add up to great good over a lifetime.

By now, you're absolutely committed to doing and being everything in alignment with The Tap; you expect it of yourself in every situation and under every condition. Whereas Stage Six could be characterized as sharing your blessings for the sensational good of it, Stage Seven is more about purposeful good. There's no self-congratulation at this level. It just is.

You experience a 360-degree sensitization to The Tap, where the action in response to a Tap Moment comes almost as quickly as the awareness of it. You seek, pray for, and create your own proactive Tap Moments. You realize that you've become a channel for the good of others, that your actions facilitate the flow of God's blessings *through* you, not because of you. The most important progression through Stage Seven happens when you've become a conduit for other people's Tap Moments. You become a teacher and leader of a growing Tap army. Other people who are moving up the spiral seem to surround you all the time.

The Stage-Seven response to The Tap: *Thank you, God, for the awareness.*

Stage Seven can be likened to a black belt in martial arts. It denotes a certain mastery of basic concepts and a skill level well above the uninitiated. But it isn't a particularly mysterious or daunting process to earn your black belt. Most people do it in about three to six years through discipline and applying what they learn. It doesn't depend on some mystical anointing or a lineage of special abilities.

Similarly, you can achieve The Tap's Stage Seven—and do it a lot faster than in three years' time—by doing what you now know, answering the call when it comes, looking for opportunities to share what you can. Also be ready for each new stage of The Tap to have its tests: prepare yourself to confront and pass them by applying what you've learned in this book.

It's possible that you'll experience progress only to slip back a stage or two, even in the course of a single day. This isn't like ascending a ladder, where you go hand over hand and climb up the rungs. You may instead go two taps forward, and then one tap back. Still, you'll benefit most by training your mind to think in the ways of the higher stages; spinning up and down the spiral, particularly in the lower four stages, can lead to despair and depression, feelings of emptiness and hopelessness, where the seven deadly distractions run rampant through your day.

However, once you've reached Stage Five, you're likely to find that you don't often dip below that baseline any more. From there on up, each stage gain is also more apt to be sustained. By the time you reach Stage Seven, you may find that you never leave, unless you get seriously distracted. (Remember the "seven deadly distractions.") At Stage Seven, you also begin a new progression; as in martial arts, the first-degree black belt initiates another series of lessons. You may progress through many more degrees at this level of mastery.

Are you ready to earn your black belt in the spiritual arts? As soon as The Tap becomes the fabric of who you are, once it surrounds you and circumscribes your entire life, you become highly attuned to everything that's around you, you have a calmness that comes from within, you abandon fear and observe the world in a different way. You fully understand the power that is in your hands.

YOUR CHAPTER 13 *Tap* MOMENTS

• Realize that none of these stages is bad, although each graduation to a higher level represents a decidedly greater understanding, appreciation, and integration of your Tap Moments.

• Where are you now in the upward spiral? What will it take for you to get to the next level?

• Understand that after reading this book, even after reading just this one chapter, you can find yourself in at least Stage Five, then move very quickly to Stage Seven, and stay there!

Fourteen

STRAP YOURSELF IN: PREPARE FOR THE RAPID RATE OF ASCENT

SOME OF MY MOST vivid memories of my preadolescent and early teen years are from when I would sit, transfixed and less than two feet away from the screen of our fifteen-inch black-and-white TV, watching Evel Knievel on *ABC's Wide World of Sports*. As the "world's greatest daredevil" attempted death-defying motorcycle jumps, he earned my total fascination.

Oh, how I wanted to be him.

One chilly Sunday afternoon when I was twelve, I watched him jump over thirteen double-decker buses in Wembley Stadium, crash-land his Harley, and then get launched off of it to go tumbling for more than fifty yards in one of the most spectacular smashups I'd ever seen. Then Evel Knievel got up, composed himself, addressed the crowd, and *walked* out of the arena despite numerous serious injuries. Excited, I sprinted outside to reset my own ramp, tossed aside the measly ten bricks I'd stacked underneath it for my prior jumps, and replaced them with a three-foot-tall metal trash can. This would give me greater distance, yet more danger. *Perfect.* Inspired by what I'd just seen on TV and my hero's "feel the fear and do it anyway" approach to life, I grabbed my Schwinn bike with its banana seat, slammed my Pee Wee football helmet on my head, and raced up the driveway on a steep hill in our back yard. I even tried to paint one of my Fruit of the Loom T-shirts with the crossed red, white, and blue insignia Evel always wore as part of his costume.

As I sat trembling on my bike at the summit, I imagined I was the man himself, at the top of his ramp inside a London stadium with close to a million cheering fans.

With my heart racing and mouth dry, I pedaled and sped as fast as I could toward my steep takeoff. While a friend watched, I hit the more than 45-degree incline and launched what must have been ten feet above him. I looked down, way down, at my friend's face and saw his total amazement. For what seemed to be an eternity, he was so far below me as I sailed through the air, and then I landed with such force that I cracked all the welds on my bike frame (probably cracked a couple of other things, too). I'd ruined my bike but made the jump. Just like Evel!

It was an afternoon I'll never forget, moving through my fear and taking on a new challenge while I pretended to be one of my heroes. It cemented my admiration for the person who completely defined the word *daredevil* for me. Much later in life, when the *Wall Street Journal* referred to me as a "maverick real estate daredevil," I felt unworthy of the comparison but blushed with the honor, nonetheless. I'm proud and even fortunate to say Evel Knievel's life influenced how I choose to live mine. I'm now aware that he taught me a behavioral pattern when I had no idea I was learning one.

No doubt Evel inspired legions of kids to attempt crazy stunts in their back yards. Probably none too few wound up with broken bones and frantic parents. Yet the most enduring message, his legacy from an amazing career, isn't about performing stunts; it's about conquering fear. After all, he probably crashed more often than not, so Evel's technical skill was never as riveting as his great courage. When he was recalling his most famous jump ever, an attempt to jump his Skycycle over the Snake River Canyon in Idaho, he reportedly said, "I didn't think I even had a fifty-fifty chance to make it. Everyone told me not to do it, but I was determined to keep my word, so I climbed up and got strapped in. When I punched that power button I thought, 'God, here I come.'"

He climbed up and got strapped in. He knew the stakes, he was scared, and still he followed through. His crash in the canyon takes nothing away from the fact that he prepared himself without knowing if it would be enough, acted on faith, accepted the very real possibility of death—and did it anyway. It's also intriguing to note that in his later years, he became a man of intense spiritual conviction. Always one to energize a crowd, when he made a public testimony about his faith at the Crystal Cathedral on Palm Sunday in 2007, hundreds of people came forward to be baptized.

We can learn a lot from those who embrace fear, then slowly expand their tolerance for risk—higher ramps, bigger things to jump, greater meaning, and more people to inspire—and succeed in life because they chose to do so. What most people feel when they're anticipating following through on a Tap Moment echoes the sensation Evel had when he was steadying himself to jump the Snake River. Your next Tap Moment might not be as intimidating as vaulting over a several-hundred-foot drop (on a vehicle that failed all its test runs, by the way), but your feelings of uneasiness will be no less real than Evel's were. For any sane person, there's an acknowledgment that it might not work, it might not really help anyone, you might look ridiculous, you might even wipe out. **The thing to remember is that it's no failure if you crash; it's far better to regret what you *do* do instead of what you *don't* do.**

When you decide to move forward despite your fear, you're acknowledging The Tap and saying, "Yes, I'm up to the task. I'm willing to accept the responsibility and the risks." It doesn't mean that you'll always do it perfectly. It does mean that you're going to keep moving forward no matter what.

Your Prayers Are Answered

THERE WILL BE times in your life, as there have been in mine, when the rate of ascent is a lot faster than you're prepared to handle. You're growing faster than ever, doing more than ever, sharing more than ever. The steep upward trajectory can be exhilarating and intoxicating, but some of what happens on the way up can also be completely disorienting.

Back when our oceanfront mansions first began to sell very quickly, my profile and brand was on the rise. The star was shooting. That kind of exposure breeds contempt, especially from those who aren't rising as fast. At the time, many people wanted a piece of what I'd worked so

hard to attain. I was attacked in the press for being egotistical, unorthodox, uneducated, for breaking the rules, for supposedly building my
tree house without proper permits, and for committing other petty
grievances.

For a while, it threw me into a tailspin of self-pity, and I'd pray, "God,
save me from all this. Why is this happening? I thought I was doing
everything I was supposed to do!"

Soon, though, I realized that this was *exactly* what I'd prayed for in
the first place. Maybe I hadn't explicitly asked for the hangers-on and
the bad press, but I could see that this came with the territory I expressly
desired. **With greater influence and material wealth come people who
will question your success, find you lacking somehow, and try to take
away at least some of what you've built.**

Yet I could practically hear God reassuring me, *That's just the fact of
it, Frank, and you'd better get used to it or else decide you're going to play
on a smaller field. You asked for it, you listened, you felt The Tap, and you
acted on it. It's a package deal. If you're not cut out for it, then show me
that. Show me that you're not ready for the next level, and we'll just idle
here for a while until you're prepared to realize this is all part of what
you've prayed to receive.*

There's no whining. No "woe is me." The only prayer appropriate to
the situation is to say, "Thank you, God, for showing me this. I understand why these things are happening: The territory just got a little broader.
I prayed for this on my knees, and now it's happened. Thank you!"

Regardless of the kind of "more" you're seeking in your life—in business, in your personal finances, in your family, or any other area—the

same phenomenon will prevail. There will be trials that come along with the triumphs. Remember when you got your first car? Not only did it bring you freedom, pride of ownership, and some level of "cool," but it also brought you the costs of insurance, gas, upkeep, and a greater sense of responsibility.

When I turned sixteen, my parents gave me a very nice used Camaro Z28, with an extremely powerful 400-cubic-inch engine. What were they thinking? I abused that car on the very first day I received it by taking my then ten-year-old sister Madeleine out to a church parking lot and doing burnouts and donuts until there was little left of my tires or transmission. Of course my little sister had to tell Mom and Dad of her exciting time with big brother Mickey. It wasn't a week later that the car was returned to the dealer and I was back on my moped, permanently. No triumph comes without its trials—and sometimes I've failed the test.

Think of anyone who longs to be a parent. When prayers are answered, does the child never misbehave, never get sick, never make her parents' life difficult in any way? Of course, the child does all those things and more. It's part of the job description to embrace all of this along with the joys of parenting. You may dislike what's required of you in the moment, but if you can see it as part and parcel of the good that God has placed in your life, then it eases the burden, doesn't it? It's wise to remember that it's the same with every great blessing: **Every success contains its adversities, and you can be grateful for both.** Preparing for success and adversity as best you can, and accepting them gracefully even when they surprise you, is just one more way of demonstrating that you are worthy of The Tap and the blessings it brings.

Watch Your Step

IT'S IMPORTANT TO acknowledge that many of the mine fields that come with an enlarged territory are set by you and you alone. You can check the news almost any day of the week and find people who've made some major misstep—indiscretions and affairs, rules violations, illegal activity of all kinds, addictions and abuses—that derails their success, at least for a while. These are the self-imposed land mines, where people's own weaknesses blow up in their faces. It takes a high degree of self-knowledge and discipline to avoid this kind of explosion, especially when escalating amounts of money or influence or power can give you unfettered access to the very things that would take you down.

You might be thinking that this is easy for me to say; after all, I'm a self-confessed "nerd" who goes to bed early, doesn't drink or smoke or womanize, doesn't even overeat or oversleep. Maybe my temptations aren't all that, you know, *tempting*. But I've chosen not to participate in the big distractions because I know myself. I know that if I were to allow myself to go down any of those roads, I might not come back. My addictive personality is a danger to everything I love about my life, so I moderate it; I don't indulge in things that could trigger an unhealthy obsession. My participation in events like the Badwater or the occasional demolition derby straddles the line. Of course, I wrestle with personal demons, just like everyone else, although at this phase of my life, I'm shedding some of the last (I hope) of my major temptations. My appetite for adrenaline still has the potential to get the better of me, so I need to watch myself and keep certain tendencies in check. That's part of the reason I sold all my motorcycles last year. I couldn't run the risk of tempting myself into riding so fast I'd get tickets again, which would probably be front-page news with some cheesy headline: "Local Mansion Mogul Learns New Meaning of 'Big House' After Racing Down Residential Road at 105 MPH." And then bang! My reputation would be shot. Never mind what could happen if a blue-haired little old lady pulled out in front of me, which could either leave Nilsa and Laura on their own (with me dead or in prison for causing a fatality) or caring for me as an invalid. It's clearly not worth it, so I got rid of the bikes. Heck, the zero-to-sixty time for any one of the three cars I now own (the Honda Insight hybrid and my two Yugos) is *never!* Forget tempting fate; I didn't want to tempt myself any more.

The young athletes who land huge contracts because of their physical prowess are smart to defuse their own ticking time bombs. Don't you especially respect the one in a hundred who says, "You know what? I used to hang out with you guys—and maybe I can do that again when my career's over—but for now, I need to lay low. I can't risk running across a cop who takes issue with my big salary after I've had just a couple of drinks with you all. A fraction of a point over the legal limit, and my career would take a major hit. It's not worth it. So I have to clean it up for now, guys. I hope you understand."

Such a person should be congratulated and encouraged. On the other hand, when I see people who are allowing themselves to be enticed by their own weaknesses, I wish I could warn them: "Hey, keep an eye on yourself . . . Keep yourself in check. You're succeeding but you've got the tendency to throw it all away. . . ." We all do. **No one is**

born knowing how to handle an abundance of anything gracefully. The act of managing abundance is wholly unnatural. Each of us is bound to make mistakes, to sin. So you're wise to mitigate that as best as you possibly can.

Realize that the higher the profile and the larger the territory, the greater the chance to step on one of your own land mines or to trip over one that's been set by someone else. Unintended errors can be blown out of proportion and blast your reputation, so as you take this rocket ride associated with The Tap, know that you need to be increasingly diligent in your oversight not only of your personal habits but also of the ethics and care with which those around you conduct themselves. Their mistakes can reflect badly on you, especially if someone is looking for a way to take you down a notch.

Because I've been blessed with the media's desire to cover many aspects of my life, which helps me promote both my personal brand and the Caring House Project Foundation, I'm also under their microscope. For the most part, that's okay; I don't have anything to hide. But I've had my taste of what it's like for a slipup to hold the potential for public devastation, like when a reporter discovered that we hadn't filed a very important form for our foundation one year. By the time she found out about the clerical error, the paperwork was already substantially in arrears; our thirty-day grace period had passed long ago, and we were in danger of losing our 501(c)(3) nonprofit status. Maybe it's fortunate that the reporter discovered the problem, because otherwise I might never have known about it, but it was also nerve-racking to realize that, should the reporter have decided to paint this a certain way, it could have looked as if we were unscrupulous. Of course, we addressed the issue as soon as I heard about it, and the reporter wrote a follow-up story on how quick we were to rectify the oversight, so you could say that was only a minor detonation. But can you see how it could have ruined our credibility, jeopardized our ability to raise money for our projects, and even shut down our operations altogether? It was an important heads-up for me: Now I'm more diligent about everything when it comes to properly filing paperwork associated with our growing charity, like getting our donor receipts out immediately and always watching our overhead like a hawk.

As The Tap rapidly accelerates your growth and expands your territory, be sure to look around you. **Where are all the potential traps and trip wires?** What can you anticipate, based on what you know about yourself, your business, your colleagues, your competition? Where are the potential pitfalls and your personal mine fields?

Your Mountain to Climb

I FIRST RAN across the passage below when I was reading Jon Krakauer's *Into Thin Air,* but it's actually from an older book called *Everest: The Mountaineering History* by Walt Unsworth. It speaks so strongly to those of us who are willing to put ourselves out there, to do something difficult, and to persevere because the ultimate objective is completely worthwhile. I've added a few words in brackets just to draw the close correlation with The Tap, and emphasized the most important bits in bold:

BUT THERE ARE MEN [special people] for whom the unattainable has a special attraction. Usually, they are not experts: **their ambitions and fantasies are strong enough to brush aside the doubts which more cautious men [people] might have**. Determination and faith are their strongest weapons. At best such men [people] are regarded as eccentric; at worst, mad.... Everest [The Tap] has attracted its share of men [people] like these. **Their mountaineering [spiritual] experience varied from none at all to very slight**—certainly none of them had the kind of experience which would make an ascent of Everest [Tap Moments] a reasonable goal. **Three things they all had in common: faith in themselves, great determination, and endurance.**

Yes, the air gets thinner with greater altitude, and the number of climbers dwindles as you go up. The cliché is that it's lonely at the top. But is it lonely with The Tap? Only in the sense that you're set apart by different standards and intentions than most other people have.

Some people try to cut down those who seem to be reaching higher than the rest of the crowd. In some parts of the world, they describe this as the "Tall Poppy Syndrome," the idea being that occasionally a flower will stand out because it's grown a longer stem than the rest—and the collective socictal impulse is to lop it off to level the field. You've probably experienced that in some form or another already, and you need to know that the greater your territory, and the taller you grow, the more likely someone is to want to cut you down to size.

The higher you go during your rapid rate of ascent, the fewer people you will encounter in that same sphere. So you need to surround yourself with those you trust, and learn to enjoy your own company. For me, that's a small circle of family and friends, although I know others in my position who have a much larger group with whom they share life's ups and downs. Either way, you need to plant yourself in a field of tall poppies, people who support you in your success, who reflect and respect your commitment to sharing your blessings with others.

The Tap provides a powerful antidote for loneliness in general; it connects you to other people in ways that those who haven't felt its power cannot possibly comprehend. It opens your eyes to how much we are all alike, how each of us has something of value to give one another, regardless of social station or economic level. This connection helps you stay grounded, putting your roots deep in the soil even as you reach for the sky.

This groundedness is a crucial element for not only *attracting* the "more" you desire in your life, but for *sustaining* it. It's a deep-seated belief that your foundation, your rock, is the spiritual connection that underlies The Tap.

This means you understand the concept of The Tap, you accept the responsibility, and you have confidence in your ability to handle more. You've been tapped because you've shown that you'll share the rewards of your success with others. You see yourself as "chosen," not because you have some superior genetics or what have you, but because you have stepped up and said to God, "Yes, please. I can handle the mine fields. I am now and will continue to be a responsible

steward of all the blessings you have in store for me."

Without this mindset, certain psychological hurdles can trip you up. One of the most common of these is guilt. Although it can spur you to action, if you indulge the emotion, it can cripple your ability to act on The Tap. When you begin responding to your Tap Moments, you're likely to confront some of the harsher realities of life.

Since The Tap calls me to serve some of the poorest people, I can say that I've indeed had to deal with some truly horrific scenes, and so have our donors and other contributors. We've seen starvation, illness, and the eagerness of families to give away their children to save the little ones from their circumstances. Once, after a particularly harrowing trip when we were returning from a village dedication in Haiti, I noticed that a woman who'd traveled with us had wrapped herself in her shawl and was staring fixedly out the window of the bus, not interacting with any of the other benefactors. A quiet person anyway, Theresa was cocooning herself to such an extent that I didn't want to intrude on her silence. Yet everyone else on the bus was talking about what the trip had meant to them, and they had all been deeply moved. So I asked her, gently, if she wanted to say anything about it.

She looked at me with incredibly sad eyes and said, "I'll have to get back to you tomorrow about this because I haven't been able to process everything I've seen."

I understood some of what she was feeling, had felt the same way from time to time myself. The trip home can be the hardest part. Occasionally, the contrast from my own home to the bright new villages we build then back through the desolation of the rest of Haiti can make it feel like what we do makes only the faintest ripple in the pool of desperate poverty there. So I let her alone for the time being, but when the conversation died down and it seemed everyone had shared all they had to say for the moment, I addressed the group.

"I want to warn everyone about the feelings you're going to have in the coming weeks. It will be tied to a sense of guilt you'll feel after having seen such poverty and also what just $5,000 can do to change a life here. Back home, you're probably going to have a hard time buying a new pair of shoes without feeling as if you're taking food out of someone's mouth."

I shared with them how, very often, when I returned from Haiti, the discrepancy between my life in Delray Beach and what I've just seen can feel crushing, but if I allowed it to pull me back, I would be *less effective* in making a difference for others. If I allowed my guilt to scale down my drive, my creativity, my artistry, my love for my work, then it would actually have a direct and negative impact on the people who had so moved my heart.

Afterward, Theresa thanked me for speaking plainly about the shame you can feel when you connect with the incredible hardships of some people's lives. She had been asking herself, *Why should I have it so good?* Which isn't a bad question—it can compel you to take action when you've been lazy or reluctant to share in the past. Yet it's a debilitating question if you take it too far. Theresa told me that she had been feeling as if her life was somehow "a giant waste," that she wasn't worthy of it all, and she said, "The homes built over sewage, the smell of the sick and the dying, the children eating mud patties and walking around on

Our First Haitian Village

This was a special day: Caring House Project Foundation donors and I recently revisited the very first village we ever built in Gonaives, Haiti. We began here in 2003. In 2002, we had built in Nicaragua. When someone congratulated us for helping the area's second-poorest country, I asked which one was the poorest, and we've been in Haiti ever since.

glass with no shoes on—and tugging on me constantly, not to get anything from me but some hugs and a few Beanie Babies . . . I was feeling like packing my bags and moving to Haiti so I could take care of these children full time."

Yet, after our conversation, she was starting to come to a better conclusion: *There isn't a moment in my life that I perceive as debilitating that is even remotely so.* A new perspective was dawning, and things like a flat tire, missing her favorite TV show, no signal for a cell phone, even problems with people at work or in her family shrank in importance. She was starting to see a new level of meaning in her life. The people she'd met in Haiti had shown her hope and happiness, a joy and sparkle in their eyes that we rarely see in our so-called first world. They showed her that what she could share would make a profound difference in their everyday lives, and in doing that, they had given her a gift more precious than anything she could possibly buy for herself back home.

The guilt comes from being too self-centered and too selfish with our resources, focusing inward instead of outward. So stay grounded in The Tap, continue to be a responsible steward, and whatever remorse you may experience won't waylay you from your highest purpose. If you're truly tapped and you're truly called, you'll rise above any passing feeling. If you succumb to it, you're no good to those who need you most. Sacrificing yourself on the altar of guilt serves no one. So, as I told my friends on the bus, take your family out to dinner. Buy a new pair of shoes if you need them. Likewise, I'm not going to feel guilty if I fancy a Yugo or want to take my family on a trip to our house in Colorado. You and I can be comfortable in our own skin by knowing that the limited blessings we enjoy are being shared properly, diligently, constantly.

Overcoming the guilt-driven motivations of the earlier of the seven stages of awareness (Theresa's initial response was classic Stage Three) is the very thing that propels you into living at the highest levels. You don't leave your deep feelings for others behind; they transform into true compassion, a desire to do more than feel bad about what others suffer, to *do the best you can to help alleviate their pain*. At Stage Seven, you're fully tapped into your purpose and place in the world, you see yourself as a channel for good, and you've become a willing, grateful conduit for God's blessings on others. Don't waste your time pondering who "deserves" what; instead, get moving to do what you can for those who need your help. Strap yourself in, and up you go!

YOUR CHAPTER 14 *Tap* MOMENTS

- Are you willing to try following through on a new Tap Moment, even if it might mean you'll crash and burn?

- Think back to the greatest blessing in your life so far. Have there been any adversities that came along with it? What can you learn from your experience?

- Think about your most significant 1) physical accomplishment, 2) financial achievement, 3) relational success, 4) philanthropic endeavor, and 5) health-related triumph. What traps did they lay for you?

- What potential land mines do you see in your life right now? Are there steps you can take to defuse them or completely avoid triggering them?

- What can you do today to demonstrate to yourself that obligation and guilt are no longer a motivator for you, that living a tapped life is about sharing your blessings out of love and compassion and purpose?

THE WHITE LINE FROM HELL TO HEAVEN

I LIE IN MY open casket, hands folded over my chest, eyes closed in eternal repose. A bell intones, sonorous, somber: the death knell. *Donnng . . . donnng . . . donnng . . .*

Eventually, my brother Bob stands at a microphone in a dark suit and speaks a eulogy. Some people wipe tears from their cheeks. Others have the stark, blank look of loss. A few are deeply disturbed by what they see and avert their eyes. Two leave the room altogether. My body remains motionless, as if it's empty of all that once animated my life. The daredevil is dead, and when the mourners file by the coffin to pay their respects, the room falls silent. Although some had come in making hushed jokes to cut the nervous tension, no one utters a word now.

The quiet continues until all are seated again and my voice comes, as if from the great beyond, to ask, "What do you see? What do you feel? Someday, this will be each and every one of you. You know not the day nor the hour."

Of course, I'm not really dead. But by this time, most of the people in the room have suspended disbelief and completely bought into the idea that I am, which is the point. This "leave-your-fears-behind coffin exercise" is just one part of The Frank McKinney Experience, a three-day event I host that's attended mostly by people who want to make it big in real estate. Yet it's first and foremost about expanding their beliefs about what they can achieve, why they are here, who they can become, and what they can do for others as they pursue professional excellence.

"The only thing that dies here tonight is the one fear or behavioral pattern that most significantly gets in the way of you succeeding in the business of life."

On the final day of the event, the coffin bit shakes them up thinking about their own mortality and, more important, about the life they're living right now.

When I rise from the coffin, I ask everyone to take a turn getting into that same position and imagining it as their final resting place. As each person climbs into the box and lies down, I ask, "**Are you going to be able to say you've lived your life with no regrets?** The only thing that dies here tonight, and shall remain in the coffin, is the one fear or behavioral pattern that you have identified as being the most significant impediment to your succeeding in the business of life." Remember, I ask them to identify this one fear while I am holding their hand and they're reclined in the coffin. I then ask that they make the commitment to live the rest of their life with no regrets. As they rise, they symbolically leave the fear behind, dead, ready for burial.

These are questions worth asking, worth pondering, worth answering. Perhaps the most eloquent summary of my own thoughts is this, from gifted playwright George Bernard Shaw:

⁓

THIS IS THE TRUE joy in life, the **being used for a purpose** recognized by yourself as a mighty one; the being thoroughly worn out before you are thrown on the scrap heap; the **being a force of Nature** instead of a feverish selfish little clod of ailments and grievances complaining that the world will not devote itself to making you happy....

I am of the opinion that my **life belongs to the whole community** and as long as I live it is my privilege to do for it whatever I can. **I want to be thoroughly**

used up when I die. For the harder I work the more I live. I rejoice in life for its own sake. **Life is no 'brief candle' to me. It's a sort of splendid torch** which I've got to hold up for the moment and I want to make it **burn as brightly as possible** before handing it on to future generations. *[Emphasis added.]*

Yes! When my time comes, "I want to be thoroughly used up," too. And to paraphrase some other much-quoted but anonymous soul, the objective is not to end up with as few battle scars as possible; I want to go skidding sideways into my grave, bruised and bloodied, screaming, "My God! What a wild ride!"

What about you? Surely you don't want to arrive at the final days of your life unscathed—untouched, untried, untapped. This would mean that in the end you will have risked nothing, tried nothing, done nothing except to hold a pretty white lily between your ten well-manicured fingers. This final chapter is about really living, about experiencing all there is for you while you're here. No matter what you believe about what happens after death, one thing's for sure: The greatest gift you have *today* is your life, right now.

Imagine yourself in that coffin, your head on a satin pillow, your body surrounded by pleated drapery, wearing your finest. Is there any hesitation, any regret, any fear that's held you back from giving your all? Indeed, what could be the single greatest fear that inhibits your growth, holding you back from what you may be called to do, preventing you from succeeding in the business of life?

Feel the Fear and Do It Anyway

SEVERAL CHAPTERS BACK, I told you Carmen and Harry's happy adoption story, about how they longed for a child, overcame the fear that had prevented them in the past from becoming parents, saw the risks, prepared themselves for heartache, and were rewarded beyond their expectations. Now I want to tell you another adoption story, one with a different kind of ending, but one that no less powerfully illustrates The Tap—and shows you how important it is to follow The Tap even when it seems unthinkable.

Lisa Smith-Batchen is an elite ultrarunner who is one of North America's top endurance athletes. She coached me through my training for my first Badwater Ultramarathon, and she's a dedicated fundraiser for AIDS Orphans Rising, an organization that benefits children in Africa whose parents have died of AIDS. Lisa's also a world-class mom who, along with her equally talented runner-husband, Jay, adopted their son when he was three-and-a-half years old. Until their son was five, Lisa and Jay did what all new parents do: They cared for their boy, they attached to him, they loved him, and they built a family with him and their daughter, Annabella. (Nilsa and I are blessed to be Bella's godparents.)

Then one day there was a knock at the door, and their son's birth mom announced, "I want my son back."

Faced with the manifestation of most adoptive parents' greatest fear, Lisa was admirably strong. I confess I don't think I could react so charitably. She was able to view this young woman with love and compassion, and Lisa attempted to understand the kind of loss she must be experiencing. Yet there was no question in Lisa's mind of breaking up her family. So she made a brave choice and invited the woman into their lives.

Unfortunately, this part of the story doesn't end well. The young woman's old problems resurfaced, and it was obvious to Lisa and Jay that it wasn't in their son's best interest to maintain contact. The young woman became insistent, aggressive, unwilling to take no for an answer. During this time, Lisa learned that her son had actually been adopted once before and that the first set of adoptive parents had returned the child to the agency because the birth mother had harassed them, too. Soon, the young woman was pressing Lisa's family for money, threatening to torment them unless they paid her huge sums and provided her with a home and food. They refused and moved their son into a school where the doors are locked and you can get in only if you know the security code.

Still, the birth mother succeeded in kidnapping the child and eluded the police for two weeks. When the police returned Lisa and Jay's son home, he had lice and scabies, hadn't bathed in the time he'd been gone, and had eaten only junk food.

It was hellish. From then on, the boy couldn't even play in the front yard, and the barrage of demands never stopped. Lisa began praying, "Dear God, please show us a way to keep our son safe!"

Twelve days before Christmas, Lisa answered the phone—*tap!*—to hear an accent so thick that she struggled to make out what the man wanted. When it began to dawn on her, she fell to her knees: A friend had done some detective work and found her son's birth father, who was calling from where he lived, thousands of miles away. He had never known that his son was placed for adoption. He was distraught and desperate to see his child again, whom he'd been unable to find since the birth mother had taken the boy away at ten months old. All along, the birth mother had insisted that the boy's father was a drunk, an addict, and in an institution—all lies.

Lisa gave thanks for a Christmas miracle.

The next day, the boy's father arrived in the United States, and when Lisa's family met him for the first time, they all marveled at how much the father and son looked alike. They shared other characteristics, too: kindness, a loving way, compassion, sincerity. Lisa says that the connection between them was the most amazing thing she'd ever witnessed. As the family got to know the man, they also knew what to do: Lisa's adopted child must go live with his birth father outside of the United States, outside the reach of his unstable birth mother, deep inside the protection of a father who loved his son more than anyone else on earth.

Lisa has come to see her role in her son's life (and, yes, she still regards him as her son) as that of guardian angel, a mother who helped her child return home. Involvement with her son, both as an adoptive parent and now as a long-distance source of love and support, has been an experience full of Tap Moments and spiritual growth.

Many times, leading a tapped life is about endurance, acceptance, surrender, even sacrifice. It is about pursuing deep-seated passions and life-altering paths. It keeps you in constant preparation for the next Tap

Moment, showing you how, eventually, you find yourself in a kind of "tap dance," a state of awareness and even jubilation as you recognize that the moment when things start to look most difficult is the time to get most excited about God's coming tap. In time, Lisa and Jay were rewarded for their supreme and almost unthinkable sacrifice with the completion of their family, another adoption of a beautiful girl, Gabriella.

Footfalls Across the Desert

LISA'S ONE OF the most mentally tough people I've ever met. She pursues physical feats few people attempt, much less achieve. Her athletic skill and knowledge coupled with a fierce will are what made her such an incredible coach for me during my first Badwater Ultramarathon, the grueling test of endurance and discipline that *National Geographic* and the Discovery Channel have called the "world's toughest footrace."

The race is a spiritual touchstone for me, which is why I return to its example over and over again, especially in this book that's focused on faith coupled with action. Running, walking, and dragging myself through this race has been the single best metaphor for living that I've found. Whether you're a runner/athlete or not, you can certainly relate to the ups and downs that so closely mirror life's own triumphs and trials. For me, aside from family-related events, running and finishing this race multiple times has provided me with some of my most enlightening experiences. I've shared with you how blessed I feel in the life I've been given, a life I could never have imagined and only vaguely dreamed of as a young boy. Having Badwater become a part of my being at this stage (I first ran it when I was forty-two years old) has caused me to reflect and then distill the lessons I've learned while chasing the white line from hell to heaven.

Each time I've been honored to participate at Badwater, and every other year they've held it, the race starts in Death Valley at 282 feet below sea level in mid-July, where air temperatures exceed 130 degrees and ground temps are above 200 degrees. You traverse 135 miles through the desert and over three mountain ranges, all on black-top pavement with the route marked out by a solitary white line on the road. You pass landmarks with names like Furnace Creek, Devil's Cornfield, Stovepipe Wells, and Lone Pine. It is hot. It is lonely. Running, you reach the depths of desperation and learn the true meaning of hope.

Finishing Badwater, the Toughest Footrace in the World

Photo credit: Chris Kostman/Badwater.com

Only ninety elite athletes are invited from around the world to participate in the Badwater Ultramarathon, and only about 65 percent complete the race. Here I am crossing the finish line for the third consecutive time.

Each footfall across the desert is akin to a rebirthing. The forty-eight-hour gestation period leads to a new, raw outlook on life. Your mind shifts, your body cries out, and your soul is cleansed in two days' fire when nothing else matters but your survival, your relentless forward motion, and the people who are supporting you in the race, bringing you water and food and encouragement. Your senses are heightened to a state of euphoria by the majesty of Death Valley.

In 2005, I was invited to my first Badwater. Lisa can attest that I was the very essence of a rookie; certainly, my resume was the lightest of the ninety-racer field. After a year of intense preparation, self-denial, and self-sacrifice, I endured hellish conditions to finish on July 13, 2005 in 48:49:20. I was never more content and happy in my life, and for a time, I experienced crystalline pure jubilation.

I accomplished my goal of finishing the race and told those close to me that I would never return. Lesson: **Never say never to anything in life.**

After a few weeks passed, I felt there was something missing from my 2005 experience. Those who finish Badwater in under forty-eight hours are awarded the coveted Badwater belt buckle, the holy grail of ultrarunning circles—and I'd missed earning mine by a mere forty-nine minutes and twenty seconds. If only I had run another 260 feet each hour, I could have had that prize. It didn't matter at the time, and I wish it hadn't mattered after the passage of some time, but it did.

As the date for entry into the 2006 race drew closer, I'd resolved that the training alone wasn't something I thought I could endure again.

My full real estate schedule and charitable commitments through our Caring House Project Foundation provided equally compelling reasons to say no.

Enter desire and passion. How badly did I want it? What was I willing to sacrifice? To endure? The self-denial and discipline would have to become even more intense if I decided to undertake this brutal challenge again. And what for? To shave forty-nine minutes and twenty-one seconds off my time for a meaningless belt buckle?

No way.

Yes way.

So it began. Commitment. Promise. Focus. No excuses. I sent in my application the last day they were to be received, and in short order I was honored with an invitation to return.

The training started in February 2006. I applied what I learned in 2005 to my training schedule, altering my running style completely. I ran further. Longer. Pulled the same SUV tire hundreds of times over a local bridge and back. I trained in a hotter sauna. Worked on training while sleep-deprived. I suffered more. Even made a solo trip to Death Valley prior to the race to run certain sections of the course while "crewing" for myself.

There was only one way to approach this, with the belt buckle and "Sub-48" in mind. Intense visualization, meditation, and prayer.

My crew and I arrived at the start line on July 24, 2006. With the temperature already exceeding 105 degrees, the gun went off at eight in the morning and, after a year of thinking about what could have been, I set off in my pursuit of "Sub-48." That was our mantra. We even had team shirts made up that depicted a submarine under water with the number forty-eight on it.

It didn't begin well. I arrived at the forty-two-mile checkpoint over an hour behind my time from the prior year. Meanwhile, the race was literally heating up. The mercury soared to 131 degrees. The pavement exceeded 200. One crew member handed me a peanut-butter-and-jelly sandwich that I carried for a few hundred yards before eating it. By the time I brought it to my mouth, the bread was toasted!

By mile fifty I was experiencing severe gastrointestinal problems, and by mile fifty-five I had horrible blisters (I still had eighty miles to go). By mile sixty, while climbing the first 5,000-foot pass, I was running with ice bags on my hips to try to reduce the inflammation.

Some twenty hours into the race, I tried to cool down and rest by taking off all my running clothes and lying in the back of the crew van, completely spent. Due to total heat exhaustion, I couldn't focus even a few feet in front of me. My head spun and my body shook. Nilsa tells me I attempted to speak but didn't make any sense. At some point, I stumbled out of the van completely naked, body quivering even though it was 108 degrees, crawled on the dirt on all fours, and vomited for half an hour. All fluids were lost, and likely my race was lost, as well.

Drawing from my 2005 ordeal, I knew perhaps with time and faith that this could pass, and I could at least finish. Lesson: **Regardless of the debilitating moments we face in our business, health, personal life, relationships, etc., if we just allow the passage of time and a little faith in God to cure the ailment, often we can emerge ready to conquer.**

At the time, I was unsure if I could continue. I decided to put my

shorts and shoes on and start walking very slowly as the sun came up on day two. There was no running at this point, just dragging one foot in front of the other. In this phase of the race, my spirit was nearly broken. My eyes were drying quicker than I could muster the strength to blink.

When I reached the van for our mile-ninety checkpoint, I looked at the giant picture of me crossing the finish line in 2005, which we'd taped to the side of the vehicle. Beneath that picture was Psalm 121, verses 5 and 6:

THE LORD WATCHES OVER you—
the Lord is your shade at your right hand;
The sun will not harm you by day,
  nor the moon by night.

I would glance at this often for motivation as the van passed.

While I was dreading another day of blazing heat, something unusual happened. In the middle of the desert, a few dark clouds started to form at mile 95, one just overhead. This cloud stayed with us and, while still hot, protected us from direct sun for hours. A gift from heaven.

As we passed the one-hundred-mile mark at 3:30 in the afternoon, we celebrated by having the crew douse me with silly string. With thirty-five miles to go (only a marathon and a half), we were gaining on lost time. We were picking up the pace. I had made it through a very low point.

At mile 105, the sky turned even darker and began to rumble. Lightning was striking within a few hundred yards. Then it happened: a downpour of a magnitude rarely seen in Death Valley. The rain drops turned to the size of peas and every other one froze into a pellet of hail. Welts began to appear on exposed areas of my body. Oddly, the temperature dropped to an unbelievable sixty-seven degrees. An incredible relief from the heat.

A Refreshing Change

Photo credit: Chris Kostman/Badwater.com

Thank God for the rain! I may have been the first ever to "swim Badwater."

The hills were unable to absorb the heavy rains. Within thirty minutes, we were engulfed in a full-blown flash flood, where washouts a few feet deep swallowed the road where we continued to run. While this may have seemed dangerous, it was a welcome change. As we crossed one intense washout I decided to do what probably no other runner in the history of the race has done, to "swim Badwater." I dove into the current as it passed over the road and actually swam for a few minutes. Now, we were having fun.

I'd never felt better. The rains stopped as quickly as they came. As the daylight hours waned on day two, I was rockin' to heavy metal on my MP3 player while I sprinted with a friend—yes, *sprinted*—across the desert, singing and throwing stuff. We still had a full marathon to go, but I don't think I ever had more fun running in my life as I did in the last three to four hours of daylight on July 25, 2006.

For the last thirteen miles of the race, I wondered, *Could I make it?* The elevation climbed from 2,500 to 8,500 feet—this after I'd endured 122 miles. *Would we cross the finish line in under forty-eight hours?* All of the excitement of the storm and the sprinter's pace of a few hours before had completely sapped my energy. I was not used to the elevation, and I began to get very dizzy and short of breath.

The pressure on my blistered feet was magnified by the steepness of the grade. My feet were now bleeding, but no way was I going to risk stopping and perhaps cramping. At a pace of two miles per hour, I trudged toward the finish line. It was well after midnight, and there were so many stars that there was more white than black in the sky.

When we had only a few miles to go, the temperature dropped again, and I was in the midst of a slow death march. One of my crew, Jill, stayed with me, and would turn off her headlamp every so often so we could see the shooting stars. Finally, the last mile. I almost didn't want it to end. Lesson: **Life's pursuits are always about the journey, not the destination.**

Except for Jill's light, it was black-hole black, and then around what seemed to be an unending number of switchbacks came a faint glow that grew brighter as we approached.

Could it be?

It was the finish line.

Our entire crew and my daughter, Laura, and my mom, Katie, joined us for the final sprint to the line. With tears streaming down our faces, we broke the tape as a team. It was the team who got me there, and they were going to finish with me, all eight of us together.

I fell to my knees, overcome with emotion. I looked at my watch, and yes, after nearly two years of training and sacrifice it read 43:02:40! I did it. Actually, I crushed it by nearly six hours over the year before!

The hard work, the desire, the passion and self-denial resulted in me meeting the most significant personal challenge and achievement of my life so far.

As I've said before, we all have our own Badwaters, our own goals and aspirations that lay themselves on our hearts. They pierce mere desire and result in passionate and "tunnel-visioned" pursuit. Are you willing to understand and commit totally to whatever your Badwater represents?

Before running Badwater, I'd never heard of an ultramarathon or even run a half-marathon. Similarly, before undertaking my first fixer-upper in 1986, I had never been involved in real estate. Before our first million-dollar spec home I had never sold one over $200,000, and there has never been a nine-figure oceanfront spec home ($135+ million) like the one we will build.

Each new frontier takes an unwavering commitment to the pursuit. Relentless forward motion. Creative persistence and perseverance. Never giving up and giving the pursuit enough time to produce the desired results. Taking the "lunch pail approach."

My life's aspirations may be nothing like yours. Yet any and every time you take the incomprehensible and turn it into the possible, the same kinds of dedication and courage are required. Whatever the "incomprehensible" thing is, everyone goes through peaks and valleys, the dry desert and the lush mountains. Everyone has the opportunity either to respond to The Tap or to turn away. Everyone has the choice of seeking out the familiar and the comfortable and the mundane and the unfulfilling—or to face their fears and go for it.

Don't compare yourself with me or anyone else, nor your achievements with mine or anyone else's. As it says in the famous poem "Desiderata" (Latin for "desired things"),

If you compare yourself with others,

you may become vain or bitter,

for always there will be greater and lesser persons than yourself.

Never dismiss your efforts as smaller than, or inflate them as greater than, those of the people around you. I have no illusions that my own Badwater experience, although each race has challenged me to my limits at the time, demonstrates the limits of humankind.

When I run, I raise money for the Caring House Project Foundation, and I also experience intensely personal epiphanies. Like the "marathon monks" of Mount Hiei, Japan, I run for spiritual enlightenment. I don't, however, run with the same austerity and rigor as they do. Instead of Nikes or ASICS, they wear sandals made of straw. They carry books, directions, mantras, food, and candles as they go. They have no crew to support them. They eat very little and make so many stops at temples that they don't have much time to rest or recuperate. During the final test of their endurance, a two-year trial of running the equivalent of two Olympic marathons *every day for one hundred days at a time,* they carry with them a sheathed knife and rope, the "cord of death." If they cannot finish their ultimate test, they end their misery on the side of the road by hanging or eviscerating themselves. Yet there have been no deaths among the marathon monks since the nineteenth century. The men prepare themselves for this final course for five years, undertaking Buddhist training in meditation and calligraphy, and performing temple duties, plus the *doiri.* This *doiri* is a seven-day fast with no drink, food, sleep, or rest of any kind, so severe that a monk emerges from it with many of the symptoms of death. Monks report a feeling of "transparency" after this feat, where they claim incredible clarity about the nature of human existence, as well as unsurpassed sharpness of the senses.

It makes you rethink just what we're actually capable of doing, doesn't it?

Tales of this kind of human strength and capacity for what a person can endure might make you start to think these men are saintly from the start. But don't forget that the marathon monks train for five years before they embark on the most punishing final two-year test. They certainly are extraordinary; only forty-six men have completed this 1,000-day challenge, spread out over seven years, since 1885. But they also certainly experience the same obstacles that the rest of us do when attempting something that appears impossible. For the person who's never run so much as a mile, doing so can seem unthinkable. For someone who hasn't earned the income he or she desires, doing so can seem unachievable. For anyone who longs for anything that's yet to be, doing so can seem unreachable. But all is within reach with The Tap.

What passions or pursuits drive you? Forget anyone else's accomplishments or desires. Are you willing to say yes more than no to your own unique calling? Celebrate each humble victory as a triumphant achievement along the way? If so, take the risk, and awaiting you will be your own belt buckle, or better.

Remember that any of life's meaningful endeavors follows a course not unlike the physical trials I've described to you in this chapter. Think about your relationships, your professional pursuits, your beliefs or philosophy of living, your engagement now with The Tap—anything that you consider important. You probably started out with a kind of giddy infatuation, and in time, you started to encounter difficulties. If you had the discipline and endurance to stick with it, you learned the invaluable lessons of how to deal with those difficulties. You now realize that more of the challenges that you face are created in your mind than in reality, and that this is where you have the most power to change things. Your fears can grip you, or you can overcome them. You can let their hold on you grow tighter, or you can face them and break free.

You can succumb to self-doubt and perish, or you can find a way out and flourish.

When I was training for my third Badwater race, I hit the wall. Despite the prior years' successes, my confidence evaporated. On one of my runs, I cursed the race and threw my water bottle into the ocean. My weight dropped to 169 pounds, which on my six-foot-one-inch frame is ridiculously thin. What was at the bottom of this? An intense fear of not finishing the race. For some reason, although I'd done it twice before, the irrational fear took hold and shook me by the neck. I began to feel as if I'd rather die than not finish—like a perverse marathon monk, I'd begun killing myself before the race began.

Facing this fear meant exposing my faulty thought process and intense feelings of self-doubt. I even went to see a sports psychologist. Although I had only one visit, it caused me to reflect on a few important lessons learned and approaches I can use in my life: 1) Just as in my prior Badwater races, when I was at the depths of physical and emotional despair, with faith in God, the passage of time, and perseverance, the debilitating moments would pass; 2) simply, I signed up and I am not a quitter, so I needed to take my "man pill" and deal with these feelings; and 3) all I needed to do was picture myself out there in the desert, with all its beauty. Fortunately for me, I tended to recall the highlights of past race experiences, not the low ones. In the end, it was all for naught. I made it through Death Valley, although struggling mightily. I ran the race. I earned the coveted Badwater belt buckle again.

At the end of any "race," you may say, "Never again!" The pain may be great. You may be exhausted. But then time passes, and you have faith, and the will to run can come back again. You're called to focus on the best and brightest, not to languish in your past, most desperate moments. As you run the next race, keeping your mind on what makes you strong, confident, and moving forward will propel you down the road.

What you're reading in this last chapter should raise important questions for you, even if you never plan to lace up and hit the pavement:

- How far are you willing to go for what you believe in?
- To what lengths are you willing to sacrifice?
- How much will you endure to attain a significant pursuit?
- Or, as I've asked before, **how badly do you want it?**

When you're faced with what seems to be an insurmountable challenge, will you accept it? Will you face your fears? Are you willing to endure purposeful training along your own white line from hell to heaven? Will you prevail over the setbacks associated with the pursuit of succeeding in the business of life?

This book began with the simple idea that everyone wants more out of life and that whatever your "more" is, there's a God-anointed pathway to it. *From those to whom much is given, much will be expected.* Now that we're nearing the end of *The Tap*, you probably have a clear view of how great the expectations may be and how faithful you must become. Do you accept the challenge? Again, I have to ask, how badly do you want it? There is no wrong response, only deepening levels of desire found from answer to answer.

What's Next for You?

LET ME URGE you now to move on from these pages. I certainly hope that this book has already provided you with many Tap Moments of your own, sparking enthusiasm and anticipation for what's next for you. You're primed to move beyond this book—this "coach," if you will. The first year that I ran the Badwater, I depended greatly on Lisa to get me ready for it. She prescribed my every move from September 2004 all the way through the race in July of 2005, and I constantly reported back on how I did. It worked! I finished the race.

In the subsequent attempts, though, I went it alone. I decided to grow beyond my coach. I took what I had learned from her and then put the responsibility of continued improvement on my own shoulders, right where it belonged. Nobody knows me as well as I do, and so I created my own program of training for myself, based on self-knowledge and my intent study of what Lisa had taught me. I may not have an advanced education, but I am a lifelong learner—I know how to integrate lessons and then apply them to accelerate my own growth. I have faith that you can do this, too.

Commit yourself to being a learner rather than a student. You know the difference? Learners apply what they know; students just keep going back for more knowledge. I'm sure you know some people in both categories. I often meet perpetual students when I give an address at someone else's event, people not-so-kindly referred to in the business as "seminar junkies." The seminar starts to replace the action it hopes to inspire. Here's how I think that works: Let's say someone goes to an event like this, or they read a book, or listen to a tape, or whatever other reasonable source of vitamin M (motivation) they might seek, and it gets them all excited to follow through. They walk out of there saying to themselves, *Yes! I'm going to do it!* But then the self-doubt creeps in, and they let go of what they've learned, and it's just easier to resume their old ways. So they attend another seminar as a way of distracting themselves from the fact that they've let the fear get the best of them. Ultimately, this turns into just another way of saying no, a cousin to overthinking, an excuse not to follow through and close the loop.

My hope is that this book continues to inspire you in the days to come, and that all of the stories and admonitions about accepting risk and acting in spite of the fear spur you forward. It's time for you to go out on your own. Pardon the sexist language, but it's time to "take your man pill," even if you're a woman.

Certainly, I hope that you come back to this book when you need another dose of vitamin M. But I'm no great evangelist (and certainly no angel), so I won't tell you that all your solutions can be found here or that if you "lay your hands on this book, you'll be healed!" Yet I do hope my words have filled you with enough inspiration and motivation that you'll do exactly as you are called to do and without hesitation.

The Tap Moments you may have found here have been yours and yours alone. I'm honored to have been a conduit if you've sensed God's presence at any point in your reading. Haven't you felt God's finger poised above you for fifteen chapters? Now it's grazing your shoulder. It's time to stop listening to what I have to say and start listening to The Tap.

NOTES

Introduction

1. Lyrics are from "Synchronicity II" by Sting and the Police (1983).

2. Bible verse is from Luke 12:48.

3. Rich DeVos's words first appeared in *Hope From My Heart: Ten Lessons for Life* by Richard M. DeVos (Thomas Nelson, 2000), p. 103.

Chapter 1

1. John D. Rockefeller quote: cited in *The Call: Finding and Fulfilling the Central Purpose of Your Life* by Os Guinness (Thomas Nelson, 2003), p. 132.

2. Julio Diaz's story was featured in NPR's *StoryCorps* segment, March 28, 2008; also "A Victim Treats His Mugger Right" from the NPR website, http://www.npr.org/templates/story/story.php?storyId=89164759.

3. Visit The Caring Kitchen online at CROSMinistries.org.

Chapter 2

1. Bill Gates and Bono's story came from Nancy Gibbs's "The Good Samaritans" in *Time* magazine (December 18, 2005), cover story.

2. To see the sources for the poverty statistics and read more like them, visit GlobalIssues.org's "Poverty Facts and Stats" page at http://www.globalissues.org/TradeRelated/Facts.asp.

3. Anthony de Mello on worldy v. soul feelings: From *The Way to Love: The Last Meditations of Anthony de Mello* (Image Books, 1995), p. 2.

4. Frederick Douglass's story can be found in various sources, but for quick reference, see the Wikipedia entry, http://en.wikipedia.org/wiki/Frederick_Douglass.

5. "Bless me indeed, and enlarge my territory": *The Prayer of Jabez: Breaking Through to the Blessed Life* by Bruce Wilkinson (Multnomah Publishers, 2000).

6. Giving to get is trading: *Life Is Tremendous* by Charlie Jones (Living Books, 1981), p. 38.

7. World food crisis: "Hunger in Haiti Increasing Rapidly" by Marc Lacey appeared in the *International Herald Tribune,* April 17, 2008.

8. Eckhart Tolle quote: *The Power of Now: A Guide to Spiritual Enlightenment* by Eckhart Tolle (New World Library, 1999), p. 49.

Chapter 3

1. The comedy bit is from "Secret Secrets of THE SECRET Revealed" by Mark Day, http://www.youtube.com/watch?v=Et_jG58qg1k.

2. *Think and Grow Rich* by Napoleon Hill is a motivational book first published in 1937 at the end of the Great Depression. It's widely available for free on the World Wide Web.

3. For more information on Sir John Templeton and the Templeton Prize, visit Templeton.org.

4. Living on $30,000 a year (promoted by the guy who doesn't do it himself): "The Pursuit of Happiness, Interview with Peter Singer" by Ronald Bailey, *Reason*, December 2000.

5. Old Testament quote is from Malachi 3:10.

6. For more on the use of tithing in many religions, see Beliefnet.com, http://www.beliefnet.com/features/tithing_chart.html.

Chapter 4

1. To find more information on my system, see Chapter 2 of *Make It BIG!*

2. Socrates' famous quote about the unexamined life is from Plato's *Apology*.

3. "Average U.S. Home Now Receives a Record 104.2 TV Channels, According to Nielsen," news release from Nielsen Media Research, March 19, 2007.

4. Visit Food For The Poor online at FoodforthePoor.org.

5. The Bible quote is from John 9:3–4.

Introduction to Part Two

1. Read more about how too much information can muddy your thinking in *Blink: The Power of Thinking Without Thinking* by Malcolm Gladwell (Back Bay Books, 2007).

2. The Bible quote is from Luke 12:47–48.

3. The happiness study was conducted by economists Professor Andrew Oswald from the University of Warwick and Professor David Blanchflower from Dartmouth College. For more information, see "Researchers Find that Middle-Aged Misery Spans the Globe," news release from the University of Warwick, January 28, 2008.

4. The quote about regret comes from Basil Rathbone, an English actor born in South America, who's most famous for playing Sherlock Holmes in several films made between 1939 and 1946.

Chapter 6

1. *The Go-Giver: A Little Story About a Powerful Business Idea* is by Bob Burg and John David Mann (Portfolio, 2007).

Chapter 7

1. Learn more about Crayola's history by going to Crayola.com. Don't forget to pick your favorite and see what that says about you: http://www.crayola.com/colorcensus/history/current_120_colors.cfm.

Chapter 8

1. Jim Collins's research revealed that there was no support for the idea that "good-to-great" companies spent any more time on long-range strategic planning than the comparison companies did: *Good to Great: Why Some Companies Make the Leap . . . and Others Don't* by Jim Collins (Collins Business, 2001), p. 10.

2. Jack Canfield talks about the headlights metaphor in the movie *The Secret* (2006).

3. For more information on the Badwater Ultramarathon, visit Badwater.com.

Chapter 10

1. How cardiologists make better diagnoses and treatment plans with less information on their patients: *Blink: The Power of Thinking Without Thinking* by Malcolm Gladwell (Back Bay Books, 2007), Chapter 4, Section 5.

2. The classic calling story of Jesus and the fishermen at the Sea of Galilee can be found in the gospels of Matthew and Mark. The Bible quotes are from Matthew 4:19–22.

3. Henry David Thoreau's *Walden* is widely available online. You can read an annotated version with this passage by going to http://thoreau.eserver.org/walden02.html.

4. Google's simple page design was featured in *Fast Company*, "The Beauty of Simplicity" by Linda Tischler, December 19, 2007, http://www.fastcompany.com/magazine/100/beauty-of-simplicity.html.

Chapter 11

1. See the Frank McKinney action figure at http://www.frank-mckinney.com/action_figure.aspx.

Chapter 12

1. "Be a person" quote is from *The Go-Giver: A Little Story About a Powerful Business Idea* by Bob Burg and John David Mann (Portfolio, 2007), p. 92.

2. Marshall Goldsmith posted "An Exercise in Listening" in his blog on May 7, 2008 (http://www.marshallgoldsmithlibrary.com/blog/tag/caring/).

3. Cristóbal Colón's story appears in *The Power of Unreasonable People: How Social Entrepreneurs Create Markets That Change the World* by John Elkington and Pamela Hartigan (Harvard Business School Press, 2008), pp. 47–49.

4. Read more about Grameen Bank and social entrepreneurism in Muhammad Yunus's book, *Creating a World Without Poverty: Social Business and the Future of Capitalism* (PublicAffairs, 2008).

5. The lyrics to the Rush song "Closer to the Heart" were written by Peter Talbot (1977).

Chapter 14

1. Read more about Evel Knievel's faith and the mass baptism at the Crystal Cathedral: "Evel Overcome With Good" by Brad A. Greenberg, *Christianity Today,* April 2007 (Web-only, http://www.christianitytoday.com/ct/2007/aprilweb-only/115-43.0.html).

2. The quote about the allure of "the unattainable" comes from *Everest: The Mountaineering History* by Walt Unsworth (The Mountaineers Books, 2000), p. 236.

Chapter 15

1. The George Bernard Shaw quote comes from two sources: The first paragraph is from his play, *Man and Superman* (pp. xxi–xxii), and the second from his address at Brighton in 1907.

2. Learn more about the Badwater Ultramarathon at Badwater.com.

3. Read about the astonishing "marathon monks" in *The Marathon Monks of Mount Hiei* by John Stevens (Shambhala, 1988).

4. The poem "Desiderata" was written in the 1920s by Max Ehrmann, a poet and lawyer from Terre Haute, Indiana.

About the Author

For nearly a quarter-century, bestselling author, philanthropist, and real estate visionary Frank McKinney has been blessed with the ability to create art in the form of the world's most magnificent multimillion-dollar oceanfront estate homes, each set on the sun-drenched canvas of Palm Beach on Florida's gold coast.

The world's wealthiest clamor for McKinney's masterpieces, which are each inspired by exotic locales and infused with vivid imagination.

Just a two-hour flight away from these palaces, in the least developed country in the Americas, McKinney builds entire self-sufficient villages through his Caring House Project Foundation (http://www.frankmckinney.com/caring_project.aspx).

His gift and passion for extraordinary homes extends to his role as the founder and director of CHPF, a nonprofit, 501(c)(3) organization he founded in 1998, which provides a self-sustaining existence for families living in poverty in Haiti, South America, Africa, Indonesia, and the United States. The foundation develops entire communities, complete with homes, medical clinics, orphanages, schools, churches, clean water, and agricultural assets, including both livestock and crops.

The foundation started domestically by purchasing run-down single-family homes, refurbishing them, and then renting them for $1 per month to elderly people who were homeless, completely redefining "affordable housing."

Through seemingly contradictory pursuits, Frank McKinney has come to understand, live, and feel what he refers to as The Tap. In Haiti, for example, where 80 percent of the population lives on less than $2 a day and 22 percent of children won't see their fifth birthdays, McKinney's foundation works to bring home stability and security to the world's most desperately poor and homeless.

"Sure, that's fine for him—he's rich," you might be tempted to say. But he didn't start with building villages; his first tap came when serving meals out of the back of a beat-up old van to homeless families who were living under a bridge.

Before there was the treasure, or even the talent, he was tapped to share his time.

What is most paradoxical about Frank McKinney is that he graduated from his fourth high school in four years with a 1.8 GPA (he was asked to leave the first three schools), never went to college, nor did he receive any formal training in theology, religion, design, architecture, building, business, marketing, literature, or writing. Yet he is the creative force behind the design, creation, and ultimate sale of some of the most magnificent homes in the world, runs a large nonprofit organization, speaks around the world on practicing The Tap, and has now written five wonderful books.

McKinney is without a doubt one of the most visionary, courageous, and "contrary" business leaders of our time. His latest stateside creations include two of the world's largest and most opulent certified "green" homes (environmentally responsible), priced at $29 and $30 million, and even a $135 million, 70,000-square-foot mansion.

If there was a swashbuckling, modern-day Robin Hood, McKinney would be him, selling to the rich and providing for the poor. Armed with a rock star look, a disarming personality, and a willingness to attempt what others don't even dream of, McKinney has defied both conventional wisdom and the predictions of others to achieve success on his terms. Because of his prior bestsellers and the magnificent properties he builds, *USA Today* has called him "the real-estate rock czar," and the *Wall Street Journal* dubbed him "the king of ready-made dream homes."

In 2009, against common practice in the publishing industry, McKinney released three new books simultaneously: *The Tap; Burst This! Frank McKinney's Bubble-Proof Real Estate Strategies,* and *Dead Fred, Flying Lunchboxes, and the Good Luck Circle.*

McKinney lives with his wife, Nilsa, and their daughter, Laura, in Delray Beach, Florida.

Index

active faith, acting on The Tap, 10, 21, 36, 44, 51, 64, 83, 89, 120, 123, 149, 172, 213, 219

Acqua Liana, xviii, 12, *14*, 39, 130, 135

adoption, 172, 249

adversity inherent in blessings, 232

Annual Objective Plan, 173

attraction, law of, 49

Aykroyd, Dan, 134

Badwater Ultramarathon, 47, 103, 147, 212, 233, 249, 252–260, *253, 258,* 264, 266

Bible, xxv, xxix, 53, 59, 82, 111, 120, 168, 257

Blink, 167

book tour bus, xix, 163, *166,*

Bono, 27, 29, 35

branding, 128

Burg, Bob, 119, 198

Burst This! Frank McKinney's Bubble-Proof Real Estate Strategies, 155, 204

business of life, xxv, 11

cancer, 100

Canfield, Jack, 146

cardiologic diagnoses, 167

Caring House Project Foundation, xxviii, 3, 12, 39, 43, 48, 93, 118, 130, 184, 235, 255; and Frank McKinney's One Million Meals Relief Effort, 38, 212

Caring Kitchen, The, 21, 215

Chase, Chevy, 134

Christmas Carol, A, 217

Churchill, Winston, 50

Cité Soleil, 131

"Closer to the Heart," 208

coffin exercise, 245, *246,* 248

Collins, Jim, 146

Colón, Cristóbal, 205

comfort corridor, 130

compassionate capitalism, 9, 57, 188

contrarian, 128, 196

courage, 191

Crayola crayons, 142, 144

Crystalina, 39, *99,* 135

Day, Mark, 51

Delray Beach, 16

Dead Fred, Flying Lunch Boxes, and the Good Luck Circle, 70; the real story behind the fiction, 153, *154*

Denman, Tom, xix, 163

depression, 191

"Desiderata," 261

DeVos, Rich, xxvi, 10, 87

Diaz, Julio, 3, 24, 35

dichotomy, xxiv; *see also paradoxicology.*

Doebler, Doug, 93

Douglass, Frederick, 33, 35

ego continuum, 190

ego flatline, 190

egomania, 183, 185

enlarged territory, 35, 77

enlightenment, 142, 181

enrichment (vs. riches), xxix, 34

entitlement, 36; as subtext of "work smarter, not harder," 51

entrepreneurship, 10, 57, 94

environmental responsibility, 15, 135, 209

Everest: The Mountaineering History, 236

Fageda, La, 206

fear, 172, 228, 247

Florida Green Building Coalition, 15

Frank McKinney & Company, 171, 173, 198

Frank McKinney Experience, The, 246

Frank McKinney's Maverick Approach, xix, 16, 163

Frank McKinney's Ultimate Tour of Extremes, 130

Gates, Bill and Melinda, 27, 29, 35

Gladwell, Malcolm, 167

Goldsmith, Marshall, 205

Go Giver, The, 119, 198

Good to Great, 146

Google.com, 171

Grameen Bank, 207

grand unveiling, xvii

green building practices. *See* environmental responsibility.

guilt, 22, 40, 57, 239

hair, 12, 13, 88, 141

Haiti, 31, 38, 48, 81, 83, 103, 130, *132,* 240, *241*

Heinzl, Richard, 104

Hope From My Heart, xxvi

housing, most expensive and least expensive, 3, 12, 79, 129, 193

hunger, 23, 38, 41

hypocrisy, 210

Jesus, 82, 111, 120, 168

Jones, Charlie, 37

juvenile detention and jail, 8, 30

King, Don, 129, 140

King, Henrietta, 141

King, Martin Luther, Jr., 115

Knievel, Evel, xix, 227, 229

Life Is Tremendous, 37

Little, Tony, 140

lunch-pail approach, 114, 145

Make It BIG!, xxvi, 65, 90

Mandela, Nelson, 105

Mann, John David, 119, 198

marathon monks of Mt. Hiei, 262

Mayer, Marissa, 171

McKinney, Bob, 245

McKinney, Frank E., Jr., 136

McKinney, Katie, 260

McKinney, Madeleine, 232

McKinney, Laura, xxi, 111, 127, 152, 260

McKinney, Nilsa, xxi, 13, 71, 127, 152

Mello, Anthony de, 33

midlife crisis, 122

mine fields of success, 233

miracle, 8, 47, 56, 82, 251

money (what it can and can't do), 22

more (longing for, wanting), xxiv, xxvi, 5, 32, 42, 56, 122

motorcycle, Frank's jump over replica of first house sold, xix, *xxii*

mugging, 6

negotiation, 200, 203

Orlando Magic, 10, 87

Oswald, Andrew, 122

overthinking, 45, 114, 165

paradoxicology, 3, 133

parenting, 152, 172, 189, 232

perceived silence, 92

Police, xxiii

political correctness, 210

Port-au-Prince, 131

poverty, 23, 31, 38, 81, 131

Power of Now, The, 42

prayer, 5, 36, 50, 104, 159, 250; seemingly unanswered/revised, 98–101; Frank's daily, 111

Prayer of Jabez, The, 35, 77

priority sheet, 65–69

Radner, Gilda, 134

rephrasing the question, 98–101

resistance to God's will, 102

responsibility to share inherent in blessings, xxv, 24, 35, 57, 124

Risch, Karen, 149

risk, xxi, 88–92, 98, 106; risk threshold continuum, 90

Robin Hood, 3

Rockefeller, John D., 5, 58

Roddick, Anita, 192

Rush, 208

Saturday Night Live, 134

Scott, Edward (the young man in the story), 115

second acts and second chances, 28–31, 34

sensitivity to The Tap, 69–72, 90, 112, 151, 157, 223

Shaw, George Bernard, 247

simplicity, 20, 170

skepticism, 4

Smith-Batchen, Lisa, 249, 252

social responsibility. *See* stewardship.

Socrates, 68

stages in the upward spiral, 216–224

Star Spangled Banner, The, 131

stewardship, 28, 36, 37, 186, 198, 209; *see also* responsibilities inherent in blessings.

Tall Poppy Syndrome, 237

Tap Moments (stories): Julio Diaz and the mugger, 6–8; Brian and his tree-house luncheon, 12–28, 40–45; Frank seeing himself (and "himself") in newspaper, 20–22, 221; Frederick Douglass learning to read, 33; $200,000 contribution arrives amid CHPF hunger relief effort, 39; capital campaign at Frank's church, 55; Bob changing more than his job, 72–78; Doug Doebler's connection with Haiti, 93–96; assassination of MLK, Jr. encouraging young man (Edward Scott) to take a stand, 115; Jim Toner helping a veteran, 118–119; walking kids to school, 154; Jesus calling his disciples at the Sea of Galilee, 168; Carmen and Harry adopting a child, 172; in business, 187; Lisa Smith-Batchen and a Christmas miracle, 249

Telus, Fekia, 84

Templeton, Sir John, 53, 59

temptation, 233

territory. *See* enlarged territory.

Thoreau, Henry David, 170, 191

Three-Strikes-and-You're-In rule, 64, 76

time, talent, treasure, 24, 25

tithing, 54; and other faith traditions, 59

Tolle, Eckhart, 42

Toner, Jim, 118

trapped vs. tapped, xxiii, xxix

tree house, xxiii, 10, 17, *18*, 41, 72, 94

Trump, Donald, 30, 129

Unsworth, Walt, 236

U.S. Green Building Council, 15

vice (Seven Deadly Distractions), 138

Walden, 170

walking to school, 152

Wilkinson, Bruce

writer's block, 149

Yugo, 13, 43, 114, 127, 128, *129*

Yunus, Muhammad, 207

Accelerate Your Success in the Business of Life

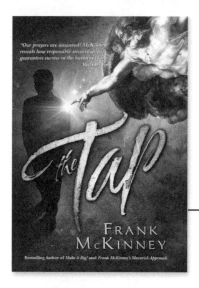

Give copies of *The Tap* to family, friends and co-workers . . .

Hardcover book (HCI, 2009)
Available at The-Tap.com • $25
Be sure to visit us online and post your story in the "Share Your Tap Moments" blog!
http://www.frank-mckinney.com/blog/your_tap_moments.aspx

Other Exciting Offerings from Frank McKinney

Burst This! Frank McKinney's Bubble-Proof Real Estate Strategies continues Frank McKinney's international bestseller tradition of delivering paradoxical perspectives and strategies for generational success in real estate. Tired of all the "bubble" talk, all the doom and gloom? Here comes McKinney in his unassailable fear-removal gear and hip boots to help you wash away the worry—the anxiety that financial theorists and misguided media constantly dump into the real estate marketplace. During his 25-year career, this "maverick daredevil real estate artist" has not only survived but thrived through all economic conditions by taking the contrarian position and making his own markets.

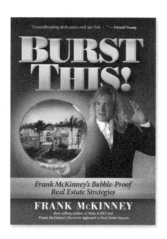

    Hardcover book (HCI, 2009)
    Available at Burst-This.com • $30

With ***Dead Fred, Flying Lunchboxes, and the Good Luck Circle***, Frank McKinney boldly enters young reader fiction in this fantasy novel charged with fairy-tale wonder, enthralling magic, page-turning suspense, and the deep creativity he's known for. It will both race and gladden the hearts of readers of all ages. This classic was inspired by real-life Laura McKinney's more than a thousand walks to school with her friends and her father, Frank McKinney.
    Hardcover book (HCI, 2009)
    Available at Dead-Fred.com • $25

Frank McKinney's Maverick Approach to Real Estate Success takes the reader on a fascinating real estate odyssey that began more than two decades ago with a $50,000 fixer-upper and culminates in a $100-million mansion. Includes strategies and insights from a true real estate "artist," visionary, and market maker.

Paperback book (John Wiley & Sons, 2006)
Available at Frank-McKinney.com • $25

Make It BIG! 49 Secrets for Building a Life of Extreme Success consists of forty-nine short, dynamic chapters that share how to live a balanced life, with real estate stories and "deal points" sprinkled throughout.

Hardcover book (John Wiley & Sons, 2002)
Available at Frank-McKinney.com • $30

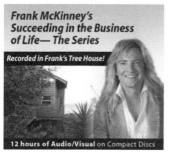

Frank McKinney's Succeeding in the Business of Life—The Series ™ was recorded in Frank McKinney's tree house by Frank McKinney himself. Twelve hours of audio and video are based on content found in his first two bestsellers, *Make It BIG!* and *Frank McKinney's Maverick Approach*, plus new and expanded information found nowhere else.

Compact Discs • Available at Frank-McKinney.com • $249

The Frank McKinney Experience, Public Speaking, Appearances and **Personal Success Coaching**
One-on-one or group events
Prices and schedule available through Frank-McKinney.com

Please visit Frank-McKinney.com to peruse our entire online store at http://www.frank-mckinney.com/entire_store.asp and take advantage of savings with assorted-product packages. It's important to note that proceeds benefit Frank McKinney's nonprofit Caring House Project Foundation (http://www.frank-mckinney.com/caring_project.aspx).